STARTUP STRUGGLES

SOLUTIONS FOR FOUNDERS & FAMILIES

MEENU KHURANA

ISBN 979-8-89233-527-0

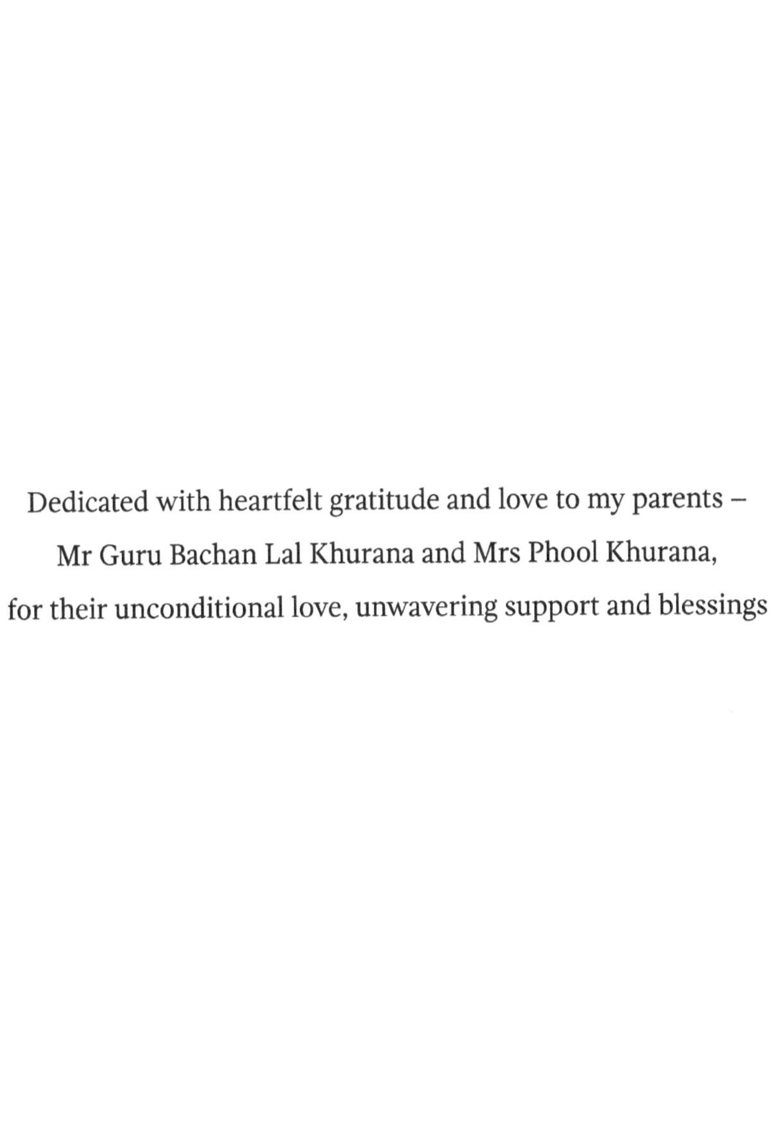

Dedicated with heartfelt gratitude and love to my parents –

Mr Guru Bachan Lal Khurana and Mrs Phool Khurana,

for their unconditional love, unwavering support and blessings

Contents

Prelude

A large courtroom on the third-floor of the district court building.

The verdict was to be out at 3:30 p.m. I had been going into that courtroom nearly every month for the past two and a half years – commuting first from Bengaluru and then from Delhi in the later months. This time, for the final verdict, my visit was prolonged by two days due to a strike on the first day and a glitch in case-listing on the second. This was day three.

On my every visit, after leaving the court, I often went out to explore the city of Amritsar. The city's vibrant culture always mesmerized me. The day prior, I visited the Maharaja Ranjit Singh Museum, recording videos of a "panorama gallery with battle scenes" for my husband, who was recuperating at the hotel due to severe back pain caused by a slipped disc. Little did I know that the events about to unfold would alter the course of my life.

This time, though, on day three of the courtroom visit, I felt differently. I felt something of a premonition. For the first-time in all these visits, I took my phone out of my handbag while waiting for Judge *Saheb* and started reading some spiritual texts to calm my nerves.

My lawyer had not sounded convincing during the morning's arguments. It came as a surprise after two years of constant assurances from him and his partner. "There is nothing for you to worry about. I am 99% sure..." he had repeated every time we raised a concern. On this visit, that stance was changed.

We, as part of a consortium of companies, had won the tender to supply Aadhaar Enabled Biometric Attendance Tablets to government offices all across India. Education departments, railways, panchayat offices, and ESI hospitals in many states have already started using our devices. However, due to the fault in the devices (from the vendor-supplied parts), we had not received payment from many of these offices and had made the hard decision to halt business and not take any further orders. As per the agreement, the "Vendor" was to provide the warranty and field support. On the contrary—and in breach of the agreement—we were refused any support from the vendor. We were sending our teams across the country to replace and repair devices at our own expense while we tirelessly sought support and assistance from the vendor.

At about a quarter past four, Judge *Saheb* summoned me to his desk. What I heard in the next few seconds would reverberate in my mind for years—or possibly for life. The court imposed on me the maximum possible sentencing and the heftiest possible penalty for cases like these. I had, for those two years, hoped to be compensated in crores for the humongous losses we had already suffered due to faulty products supplied by the vendor. Yet here I stood, with no compensation and further fines to pay. Dreams that I had nurtured for years were shattered in one moment. Tears rolled down my eyes. The Police Officer started taking down my

Aadhar details and said, at 4:45 p.m., that since the bail papers had not yet arrived, the bail would most likely be postponed until Monday. I wanted to jump off the third-floor balcony, but I never would have. I noticed the locked doors and lack of immediate access. I did, however, somehow manage to get the bail by 5 p.m. We had already missed our train and had to book a flight to return to Delhi. My niece was expected to arrive that very night to take her NEET PG exam in Delhi the following day. She was going to stay with us, and no matter the pain and turbulence, we had to go back home and put up a brave face to help support her.

The following weeks were a whirlwind. I did not sleep for eight straight days. A copy of the detailed judgment report hadn't been provided, and I couldn't consult any lawyer. Every time I dozed off, I would wake up after a few minutes screaming, asking for my mother like a small child. My children were at boarding school, and I chose not to share this news with my parents or any of my family members and friends. I felt like if I started talking about it, I'd relive the agony and break down. And that I couldn't afford that at this time. I had a long fight ahead of me.

Christmas vacation for the court was going to start, and we had only ten days to initiate an appeal in the higher court. We threw ourselves into getting the paperwork ready—and initiating a fresh appeal in a higher court with a stronger lawyer (I can say with conviction that our case was not represented well in the first appeal). My husband and the lawyer sat together for two days to draft the appeal document of 400 pages. As of the date of writing in 2023, the case is still ongoing*. The sword of Damocles still hangs over my head and reminds me to live every day to the fullest. I still sometimes get tormented by the anguish of unfairness. I cannot bear to watch any movie involving a jail scene.

"Every adversity carries with it the seed of an equivalent or greater benefit."

A quote from the book "Think and Grow Rich" became my guiding light during my days of struggle and helped me focus on the bright side of things.

There is no greater wealth than managing your own time, and there is no greater happiness than giving back to society. With these thoughts, ten years ago, I decided to walk along with my husband and join in his journey to help transform India and contribute in our small way to the growth of the Indian economy.

My story from being an employee to an employer was an exhilarating roller coaster ride, frustrating at times but a professionally satisfying journey.

---

* The case was resolved by mutual settlement by November 2023

Chapter 1

Finding Funds

"Every worthwhile accomplishment, big or little, has its stages of drudgery and triumph: a beginning, a struggle and a victory."

– Mahatma Gandhi, Indian freedom fighter and leader and Father of the Nation

Funding is like the lifeblood of a business, providing the necessary capital to kickstart and sustain its operations. It is an investment that fuels product development, team building, manufacturing, sales, marketing, and all the nitty-gritty aspects of running a business. Without adequate funding, a company can resemble a ship without a sail, struggling under the weight of its expenses. Entrepreneurs must explore various funding avenues, including angel investors, venture capitalists and crowdfunding platforms. Success in securing funding hinges on a clear understanding of why funds are needed, demonstrating a solid strategy for utilizing the funds effectively, establishing trust and the ability to present a compelling business plan to potential investors. The journey is not just about raising money but building credibility and transforming a vision into a thriving reality.

C 1.1 Fundraising Pitch

Fundraising is tough, perhaps the toughest aspect of an entrepreneurial journey for founders. Founders must secure capital for various purposes, such as hiring talent, establishing and expanding their business, generating working capital, and attracting further investment to fuel growth. Funds are pivotal in shaping your ideas and breathing life into your dreams.

To start, founders need to approach investors and make every effort possible to pique their interest. This can be achieved by showcasing their capabilities and presenting comprehensive market research reports. Where there are competitors in the same field, they must also provide reports on these competitors while emphasizing the advantages of their products/services. This approach instills confidence in investors and makes them more inclined to scrutinize your proposal. Before engaging with investors, conducting some research on them is essential. Founders should analyze the investors' areas of interest, their vision, core values, team structure, and their approach to working with startups. Prior groundwork plays an imperative role that enables you to approach situations patiently and pragmatically. It's worth noting that some investors prefer multiple meetings before making a decision. They may also request additional market reports and presentations, demanding more of your time and effort.

Investors come from diverse backgrounds, and it's crucial to personalize your pitch for each of them to make your company more appealing to their specific needs. Every investor is unique, seeking various elements in the firms they choose to invest in. Therefore, conducting thorough research, understanding your audience and determining how to best attract their attention and persuade them to invest in your company are essential steps in the fundraising process.

To play it safe, It is advisable to engage with different investors simultaneously rather than one after another. This saves time, minimizes risks and encourages investors to reach decisions more expeditiously. Founders should also assess other qualities in potential investors, such as alignment of vision, compatibility for the long-term partnership spanning 5-7 years, and their ability to offer the right guidance.

Entrepreneurs can approach investors through trusted intermediaries or portfolio companies. In some cases, investors may proactively reach out if they come across favorable reviews of your product, service, or vision. Create an aesthetically appealing pitch deck that highlights your product idea, technology, and team to investors, and be prepared to tell your memorable, authentic, and compelling story that shows your commitment and passion to the business.

If you firmly believe in your strengths, you'll be able to attract investment. The key is to continuously work on your idea and network with the right groups. Even in the face of failure, strive to garner constructive feedback. Utilize the inputs to enhance your pitch and bolster your organization's strengths and capabilities.

C 1.2 Funding Stages

Fundraising plays a critical role, especially for startup co-founders who embark on their entrepreneurial journey by bootstrapping, i.e. using their own funds, which carries inherent risks. The process of developing a Minimal Viable

Product (MVP), spanning from market research and initiation to prototyping, demands substantial effort, time, and investment. Without successfully securing the funds, there is a real possibility that their product may lag behind competitors and, in the worst-case scenario, fail to reach the launch stage. The availability of funds ensures the timely completion of the product life cycle in alignment with requirements.

Fundraising needs can arise at various stages; some startups seek funding in their early stages to establish their business, while others opt for funding when they reach a strategic juncture where they can present investors with a prototype or an MVP product, demonstrating their companies' capabilities in terms of customer base, number of employees, and skills of their team. Alternatively, some may pursue funding exclusively during the expansion phase of their company. It is imperative to have a well-defined fund usage strategy prepared before approaching investors, and it is advisable to start contemplating fundraising at least six months before the need for funds arises.

Fundraising can be accomplished through multiple avenues:

1. Founders may reach out to their network of friends, ex-colleagues, etc., and showcase their capabilities and

2. Approach angel investors and Venture Capitalists (VCs) who provide the big funding. To save time, it Is advisable to study the profiles of your VCs and ensure that they are interested in investing in an industry or technology similar to yours. The Detailed Project Report (DPR) is required to approach VCs.

The lack of funding or resources can be a significant roadblock for many entrepreneurs. There are other creative ways to overcome this hurdle. For instance, entrepreneurs can consider:

a. Crowdsourcing as a means to raise capital,
b. Collaboration with complementary businesses to share resources and expertise, thus reducing costs and opening up new avenues for growth,
c. Co-creation partnerships with established organizations.

C 1.3   Unicorns and Hype

The Indian startup ecosystem, ranking 3rd globally in terms of unicorn count, is growing fast, with 108 unicorn startups as of FY22-23. The growth can be attributed to a rise in venture capital investment, a growing young talent pool, innovative products and services, startup-friendly initiatives, and a thriving culture that values startups and entrepreneurs. The number of unicorns in India is predicted to rise 10X in the next 2-3 years. When a startup's valuation exceeds USD 1 billion, it is referred to as a unicorn. Successful unicorn founders are role models and inspire young talents to pursue entrepreneurship in every sector of the economy.

The number of startups in India until FY23 was around 90,000, with only a few designated as unicorns. While we hear a lot of chest-thumping by the unicorn founders, the agonies of startups shutting down their businesses get dinned in the noise. It's crucial to recognize how some unicorns are overvalued by investors, as many of them are not profitable and operate at losses of multiple crores. This overvaluation can stifle innovation. Unfortunately, some unicorn founders misuse funds for personal wealth accumulation. Founders must not become greedy.

Although these unicorns have garnered global interest and played a significant role in boosting the Indian economy, the pressure on new startup founders is considerable. Investors now expect the same rapid growth from every startup they put their money in. The "startup" frenzy has reached such heights that even family and friends anticipate achieving the same level of fame, wealth, and lifestyle as celebrity unicorn founders.

Startup founders must keep their foot firmly on the ground and not let performance anxiety or pressure from unicorn successes overpower their sanity. They have to make their unique journey and experience their share of achievements and failures. Founders need to understand that they are not obligated to prove anything to their family and friends. Instead, they can learn valuable lessons from others' success stories and work on developing their own strategies and roadmaps to provide the best consumer experience. They must also be realistic and reasonable. When making comparisons, they need to remember that unicorns are backed by big investors and have access to large markets. Not all startups may scale to that size, and not all founders may have the same level of ambition. Investor's caution and a measured approach to growth can help create a more stable and sustainable startup environment, ensuring long-term success.

Investors' money is safer when there is no race to enter the unicorn club. If the unicorn fails or if the bubble bursts, the entire ecosystem may collapse. Customers would face the painful effect. The personal and professional lives of founders and employees will be impacted. It may also lead to an economic downturn.

C 1.4   Bootstrapped – Leveraging Limited Resources

Bootstrapped companies are those where the promoters and directors put their own money. These are the companies that are not yet funded by any angel investors or venture capitalists due to various reasons, such as investors you approached not being interested in the particular sector/technology, didn't have confidence in your product/service idea, or the market didn't look very promising to them, etc. There could be many more reasons for startups to fail to generate investors' interest. In the absence of investors, founders have no choice but to put in their own hard-earned money and start the company. They start the company by using their savings, taking loans against properties, borrowing from family and friends, not taking their salaries, etc. They pay themselves a minimum amount – just enough to pay their bills.

Another factor that motivates promoters and directors to invest their own money is their financial knowledge and risk appetite. However, this can be a highly risky proposition, leading founders to endure mental stress for a long time. Apart from impacting their financials, their health and personal relationships go for a toss. It is not advisable to put someone's health and mental peace in danger. I strongly believe that this trait is developed during their MBA education. Business schools should reconsider their curriculum and courses in light of the case studies that explore how founders' lives are affected when opting for bootstrapping. These Business schools must caution their students of the potential repercussions of risk-taking on their lives and their families' lives. It is not easy to endure a lot of financial, physical, and mental stress for years. Weak-hearted withdraws from the world; it is tragic to lose brilliant minds in such a way.

Bootstrapped companies operate with limited funds and resources, requiring constant investment of your energies in optimizing all the resources, such as infrastructure, software, and skills. You practically have to compromise on every decision of yours. It sometimes kills your creativity, ends experimentation, and creates stress. Decisions are not governed by what is more useful for the customers or organization but are governed by the availability of funds alone, which is frustrating. On the flip side, there is a silver lining as you learn the valuable skills of how to optimally utilize all the resources.

In a startup, you find yourself wearing multiple hats – from strategy maker to social media content creator to technology program manager and more. Juggling roles like CEO, CFO, sales and marketing manager, and operations manager is a challenge. It is not the best use of your skills, and this will also result in a delay in the product launch. You also have to devote your time to looking for investors, the time which you should have spent on the core responsibilities of your job.

In 9 -to- 5 jobs, you do not have to worry about additional work and expenses such as vendor expenses, employee salaries, and various other kinds of running-the-office expenses. You can focus on your work, and you will have more time and money for your family outings, relaxation activities, family events, emergencies, and every other expense in general.

As startup founders, we had to raise funds for our business because we could not get the investment. We had to let go of all our properties in Bengaluru, a villa in Concorde Silicon Valley, a villa in Eagleton Golf Resort, a 3BHK apartment in Sobha Dahlia, and a villa in Adarsh Palm Retreat. We took a loan against our property – a 3 BHK apartment in Oceanus Triton on Sarjapur Road. We invested all our savings from US and UK stints, our Provident Funds, FDs, ESOPs, and mutual funds. We also borrowed from our families. We took a loan from market lenders at 16% interest.

There are obligations when you borrow from family, though none of them ever asked us to return money, and we never felt any pressure to return money or pay any interest. However, being in debt gives you a strange, uncomfortable feeling and a scarcity mindset. With a "lack of money" mindset, you can't focus on anything else. Whenever our families asked me, out of concern, about how the business was doing, it felt like they were asking when I would repay the money. Sharing the good news, such as buying a car or planning a holiday, made me feel guilty, as I felt we didn't deserve to spend without first repaying our debts. I'm grateful for our family's unwavering and unconditional support.

C 1.5   Success or Failure in Securing Funding

A startup needs funding for setting up the office, hiring talent, and purchasing software and technical infrastructure. Upon securing funding, you not only gain financial freedom but also attain mental peace. Now, you can focus on acquiring the best resources for your organization, scouting for better office space, and planning and implementing strategies to meet the organization's objectives. With funding, you can optimize the time to market for the product launch.

Securing funding is a long process. It requires multiple rounds of discussion with investors and their teams. The first step is to prepare a killer elevator pitch, which can be used to reach out to your prospective investors and to win their time for meetings. When we started, we had to travel a lot for face-to-face meetings. Success in securing the funding relieves your stress significantly, but it has its side effects, too. You feel that half the battle is won, so you tend to become a little lethargic. Now that you feel taken care of, you also tend to take things a little more slowly. Besides, the decision-making gets impacted because now you also have to keep investors in the loop. For any major decisions, you need to obtain their approval. Consequently, rather than spending time on creating product road maps and strategies, most of your time and efforts go into pleasing investors.

Many times, you may fail to secure the funding. Sometimes, investors do not provide any reason; sometimes, they may say you do not meet their selection criteria or that they are not interested in the product niche you are working on. Failing to find funding and investors puts a lot of doubt in your mind about product capability, your vision, your skills, and your research and analysis. Every time you face rejection, it takes you a few steps back, and you have to motivate yourself again to chase your dreams.

What do investors want? They seek strong potential in products and promoters. What problem do your product and services solve? They evaluate if there is a real demand in the market, the size of the market for growth opportunity and scalability, and who the main competitors are. Is our product more affordable with the same features, at the same price with better features, or at a higher price with superior quality compared to competitors' products? What makes your product better? They want to see your past success records, founder's and team's skills, experience, passion, and commitment. They want to determine if the business model is sustainable and profitable.

It is very important to have a firm faith in your vision and mission. At the same time, analyze the feedback provided by the investors with an open mind. Do not let the ego take over. More than the competition, ego has killed more startups. Some founders do not incorporate the feedback received and later realize that they did not understand the market correctly, even though there were clear indications from the investors.

The founders must learn from their failures, keep improving their capabilities, and keep looking for investors. They must showcase their prototypes and present their ideas with new zeal every time. Additionally, consulting business success coaches can offer valuable external perspectives.

C 1.6 Find Partners with Strong Financials

When doors do not open, it is time to check out the windows! When we did not receive any external funding, and all our personal assets and investments were exhausted, we started looking for partners with strong financial backing and shared goals, such as contributing to the growth of the Indian economy. This would ensure a partnership of equals with people who have similar interests, allowing you to give your 100% focus on the work. In such collaborations, the synergy of shared visions can often unlock new possibilities and avenues for success.

While working on various products and projects, it's crucial to actively build your network and present your ideas with a well-prepared elevator pitch to capture the necessary attention. Diligently working on your personal branding is essential. Acquiring finances is half the battle won, but the road to success is a long one. To make your journey smooth, it is important to maintain cordial relations with your partners. One must keep responding to all the queries your partners or network people may have. The success of your partner is a win-win for everyone. Coming together of two individuals/businesses with similar interests works wonders.

When seeking partners, ensure your elevator pitch is polished, backed by detailed project reports, and driven by your vivid dreams and vast vision—soon, you will attract multiple partners. When forming partnerships, ensure they are non-exclusive so that you are not dependent on just one. Keep two to four potential partners ready, envisioning it like a race with multiple horses. You don't necessarily want one to come first, but rather, you want all your horses on the ground, running as fast as they can to complete the race successfully.

The funds from our partners were utilized to establish infrastructure and recruit top-tier talent. Having financial support allowed us to develop optimal designs for our product, enabling us to concentrate on our expertise without the constant concern for finances. Additionally, we empowered our partners to build manufacturing capabilities.

This collaborative effort facilitated the co-creation of growth solutions.

If you don't find a partner with strong financial backing, the best advice is to continue your journey as a solopreneur. Begin the process with a limited capacity and keep looking for partners/investors with interest in a similar area for a smoother ride ahead. Consistency and perseverance in these efforts lead to long-term success in your entrepreneurial journey. Resilience and adaptability are key. Stay open to opportunities, and success might just be around the corner.

Months and years of hard work paid off when we secured a significant investor – a 20,000 crore company that agreed to fund our smart energy meter project. Their support enabled us to innovate, refine our skills, and enhance our capabilities. This helped us secure a very large order for 5,00,000 meters. The funds received were used to set-up the best-in-class design house and set-up world-class manufacturing infrastructure for making smart energy meters. Our vision was coming true, and excitement was at its peak. We had full independence in decision-making, hiring talent, and purchasing machines.

Over the years, we established new partnerships. We employed the royalty model with our partners, ensuring a certain amount is received when the product is manufactured. Isn't it wonderful that your partners are 100% committed, and you don't need to seek external funding? When your partners display confidence and commitment, their success becomes your top priority. These alliances have played a pivotal role in our growth journey, bringing fresh perspectives and diverse expertise to our endeavors.

C 1.7   Incredible Infrastructure of Large Companies

The infrastructure that large companies had in Bengaluru was astonishing; it felt like entering a resort when visiting with the family on weekends. However, on weekdays, the atmosphere was different – buzzing with hurried activities, individuals moving from one building to another for meetings and grappling to meet goals and deadlines. Despite the bustling activities, the well-equipped facilities provided a conducive space for collaboration and innovation.

The high-end machines, servers, networks, and systems managed various aspects, including project delivery, billing, accounts, sales, attendance, leave, travel bookings, etc. They also addressed maintenance issues, all supported by an efficient support staff, making our lives simpler. The guest houses, library, learning centers, and recreational facilities were out of this world. The landscaped gardens and lush green surroundings inspired everyone to feel proud and work hard.

The interaction we had with great leaders, expert talks, skill-building sessions, celebrations of all the festivals, and participation in national and global events helped employees feel more valued and connected to the organization. The diverse experiences enriched our work environment, promoting a vibrant and cohesive team spirit.

We had access to every kind of food, from local cuisine to global delights. A variety of dosas, Delhi chaat, Momos, Rajdhani thali, North Karnataka meals, fruit juices, sandwiches, pasta, pizza, sumptuous meals, and more! Witnessing a live roti and dosa counter, where a person effortlessly churns out 10-12 rotis or 5-6 dosas simultaneously, always fills me with appreciation for the chef's skills. At that moment, cooking at home for our nuclear family seemed like hardly any work.

When entering the startup world, the journey begins with the quest for office space. From negotiating rent, compromising on the location, planning the design, configuring the cubicle structure, and deciding on the wall and blind colors to procuring desktops, servers, printers, and chairs—every detail demands attention and meticulous planning. I vividly recall an amusing moment when my son, around seven years old, visited the office, sat on an office chair, and curiously asked, "Who bought these chairs?" When I replied, "Daddy and Mumma bought these," he quipped, "OK, Boss is the one who buys a chair for you." This became my new definition of the boss.

We also had a guest house in Delhi and Bengaluru, and we had the opportunity to furnish the house and set-up the kitchen. I still have guests asking me why there's so much stuff in the kitchen. Well, that's because, after giving away some items, the rest came to me when we discontinued the guest house facilities.

Large corporates can afford world-class infrastructure due to their extensive global client base, earnings in US dollars, and substantial profit margins. Additionally, the government supports them by offering inexpensive land and various tax benefits, especially when operating from Software Technology Parks (STP) and Special Economic Zones (SEZ).

The investment made by large companies in their infrastructure helps retain the best talents in our country, preventing them from migrating to the West. Companies can allocate some of these funds to offer improved salaries and invest more in employee welfare schemes. These enhanced facilities and benefits not only attract top-tier talent but also enable employees to focus on work with heightened creativity. Moreover, a supportive and enriching work environment through these investments contributes to employee satisfaction and loyalty. In turn, this positive atmosphere encourages teamwork, promotes innovation, and contributes to the overall success of the company.

In creating an inviting office environment, we had to forego our dream weekend villa near the Sun God statue at the Golf resort.

Chapter 2

Financial Freedom, Requirements and Challenges

"Your economic security does not lie in your job; it lies in your own power to produce – to think, to learn, to create, to adapt. That's true financial independence. It's not having wealth; it's having the power to produce wealth."

– Stephen Covey, Author and Management Guru

I always desired financial prosperity, not for flaunting but to have the freedom to pursue what I want and when I want, without worrying about the bank balance and other expenses. While money isn't the sole measure of success, it can liberate your mind from concerns. It's not the money itself that we seek; rather, it's the security it brings. Money serves as a means to give back to society. While we achieved success in developing products and executing all our client projects, the margins in electronics product design services were low, barely covering salary expenses.

C 2.1 Financial Safety and Security

We all seek financial security and safety for the following reasons:

1. Overcome overthinking about the future – Excessive worrying about the future creates stress, and if we

worry about our future, we will not be productive in the present, and the work outcome will be impacted.

2. Handle unexpected expenses – As witnessed during the Covid-19 pandemic, some families had to liquidate properties for medical treatment. Financial security is vital for managing monthly bills, education, health, family events and travel-related expenses.

3. Move forward from the past – Selling assets acquired in youth to fund a startup can be emotionally challenging. Sometimes, your heart aches as you reminisce about and long for the lifestyle and properties you once enjoyed. Although they are material possessions, owning a house is a dream, an aspiration and a fundamental need for every person. It was painful to sell off all our properties one by one to meet the ever-growing needs of our startups. Without financial security, the mind tends to dwell in the past. In contrast to the past, when credit card bills were paid promptly upon receiving the bank's message, now we were compelled to wait until the last date of payment, sometimes managing only the minimum amount. Paying huge credit card interest for months never allowed us to save any funds for emergencies. It was an awkward feeling when you try to save each penny on every expense but pay huge credit card interest. I appreciated that there was food on our plates, and we had still not lost hope.

We attain financial safety and security by holding assets in our name, including a bank balance, fixed deposits, and mutual funds, and ensuring a consistent monthly income. In the startup world, neither the monthly expenses of the office nor income are fixed. My most significant learning is that one should enter the startup world only after ensuring multiple income streams. Please do not kill any income stream or utilize it to fund the startup until the business becomes profitable and can withstand market volatility. Additionally, a newfound lesson for me is that it's time to shift our mindset and detach the feeling of safety and security from our assets. The realization has granted me much-needed freedom and peace of mind.

Startup owners must plan to consistently allocate some funds to savings and other investment avenues. It is also equally important to have a well-structured sales cycle to generate revenue continuously. Depending upon customer demand or market trends, we can explore creating new products or entering new markets with existing products. If we are not able to invest in hiring a competent salesperson, it may be prudent to stick to a 9 -to- 5 job. Before entering into the entrepreneurship journey, it is important to have built some financial safety and security.

C 2.2   Capital-Intensive Manufacturing – Setting Up and Managing a Factory

Establishing a factory involves significant capital investment, covering expenses such as machines, real estate, and resources. Acquiring a skilled workforce and planning for manufacturing shifts based on capacity, floor size, and machine availability is crucial. Procuring machines involves requesting proposals, obtaining quotes, and comparing and finalizing the vendor. Alongside this, attention should be devoted to acquiring essential government approvals and certifications.

To streamline processes and efficiently manage components and storage of ready-to-ship products, a well-established sales pipeline is essential. The pipeline ensures the continuous flow of manufacturing cycles, prevents surplus stock, and eliminates shortages during periods of increased demand. Without a functional sales pipeline, the result can be a backlog of products in storage, disrupting the entire supply chain cycle. This is a common challenge faced by entrepreneurs and could lead to financial losses and difficulty securing new orders.

Once the manufacturing cycle is interrupted, it becomes challenging to rehire skilled workers and restart operations. You have to put in the effort all over again. Therefore, the sales team must work with meticulous planning to avoid such pitfalls. There could be other issues related to manufacturing, for example, an increase in duty for the import of components, non-availability of components, currency depreciation, and withdrawal of support from chip makers, etc.

Factory setups are typically established in industrial areas located on the outskirts of the main city. Before commencing operations, it is crucial to comprehend market requirements and governmental licensing prerequisites. A comprehensive plan should be devised for procuring equipment, technology automation, implementation of quality control processes, and hiring and training workers. During the planning stage, considerations must be made for potential contingencies, including shifts in government policies, absence of a sales pipeline, lack of customers, and financial issues within the company, among others.

In addition, Include a thorough risk assessment and mitigation plan in the planning process to handle unexpected challenges. Embrace adaptability to market changes and maintain flexibility in your operational model for the factory's long-term success and sustainability.

Furthermore, building a culture of continuous improvement and innovation within the organization will enable the factory to stay agile and responsive to changing industry trends. Regular reviews of operational processes and proactive measures to address potential bottlenecks can enhance overall efficiency and competitiveness in the market.

C 2.3   Safety Net of Monthly Salary, Employee Healthcare, Life Insurance, and Travel Expenses

Your health will determine your ability to make money. If there is anyone dependent on your income, such as a spouse, children, or parents, you need health insurance and life insurance.

In 9 -to- 5 jobs, we get a salary on the first of every month, which provides us security for our future. It provides funds to pay our monthly bills, kids' school fees, and travel expenses. It helps us meet any untoward emergency expenses. Duriing my tenure at Infosys, a major fear was addressed: Infosys Foundation paid Rs 1 Cr to the family in case of an employee's death. HR head of Infosys shared the stories of how that financial support made a significant aid to the affected families. Big corporates can negotiate with insurance firms and get better health and life insurance for all their employees and their families. Startup owners buy expensive insurance for less coverage through online portals and usually ask employees to pay and contribute some amount to cover their families' insurance. All this requires an additional commitment from the startup owners and employees.

Corporate employees often stay in expensive hotels, and startups, aiming for cost-effectiveness, opt for budget-friendly accommodations. Startups manage costs by booking early morning and late-night flights and returning on the same day to save on air ticket and hotel expenses. Frequent such travel puts the founder's and employees' health on the line. Startups must devise sustainable travel strategies that prioritize both financial prudence and the health of their founders and employees.

If an organization fails to offer comprehensive life insurance and health coverage policies to its employees, they are less likely to remain with the company for the long term. When employees face medical or financial challenges within their families and find inadequate support through company policies, their satisfaction diminishes, prompting them to explore better opportunities elsewhere.

Apart from providing comprehensive life insurance and health coverage policies, startups also must ensure timely salary disbursement and offer a comfortable work-related travel experience. When employees experience regular and punctual salary payments along with convenient and well-managed travel arrangements, it contributes considerably to their overall job satisfaction and loyalty to the organization.

High overhead expenses prevent startups from generating substantial profits despite providing quality services at competitive prices. Entrepreneurs need to incorporate these expenses into their budgetary planning and strategically recruit employees committed to long-term collaboration.

C 2.4   Investment in Research Leads to Innovation

When startups invest in research, they can explore new technologies, work on innovative product ideas, and even venture into new business lines. This not only builds confidence and capabilities but also serves as a showcase for attracting new customers, top talent, and savvy investors. Smart investors often delay investment decisions to witness tangible innovation, making research investments a strategic move for startups to gain the confidence of stakeholders, secure new orders, create intellectual property, and, consequently, generate more revenue.

Startup organizations must allocate resources and budget for research work. They must identify new ideas and define research areas and objectives that are aligned with organizational goals. They must explore market gaps and emerging tech possibilities, analyze customer feedback, pain points, competitor offerings, and industry trends, and collaborate with experts. The structured approach in research leads to informed decision-making, innovation and long-term success. Our investment in research, for example, enabled us to develop smart meters, and we consistently invest in research to maintain our competitive edge.

Without ongoing research projects, organizations rely solely on customer projects, and employees build their skills on the job. This, in the longterm, leads to stagnation in the growth of the organization and its employees.

C 2.5 Demonetization, GST, Covid Crisis, Lockdown, Account Freeze by SEBI

We are living in a VUCA (Volatile, Uncertain, Complex, and Ambiguous) world. We saw the impact of demonetization, GST, lockdown, financial frauds, and SEBI restrictions. These factors were out of our control. The change in government policies cannot be predicted by anyone, and startups are massively impacted by them. The changes sometimes disrupt the operation and result in the closure of the project or product line that had a very high potential. Startups struggle to survive in such conditions. Once we understand that these factors are out of our control, we must re-evaluate our strategies, prioritize the product line and business opportunities, and take quick actions for long-term strength. Taking action and surrendering to God is my mantra to deal with uncertainties.

I've also seen that most of the employees who were doing their 9 -to- 5 jobs were financially less impacted by this. Whenever such a situation arises, keep working on strengthening the organization, nurturing customer relationships and on your personal growth. Proactive planning for contingency can help you avoid huge losses and debts.

At this point, it is important to emphasize that founders must work on building a strong foundation for their company. Startups without a strong base and strong founders are likely to collapse in such situations.

We arranged for investments from the Karvy Group for our smart energy meter products and set-up operations for manufacturing the meter under their brand, working for them on a royalty basis. We bagged an order of 5 L meters in early 2018. We successfully delivered close to 77,000 meters in 2018 and 2019. Manufacturing is a highly capital-intensive exercise and requires a sustained cash flow to keep the cycle running.

Karvy Group was badly hit by financial scandals by the end of 2019 and stopped investing in the project. All their accounts were frozen by SEBI. In the next quarter, in 2020, India had the first Covid wave, and ensuing lockdowns closed our factory for months.

We didn't know how to fulfill the order and pay for the factory worker's salary.

We burned our entire savings to help sustain our workforce for a few months and had to finally close operations. The factory was sealed, and the govt PO for the remaining 4.3L smart energy meter was canceled. A lot of people had worked for more than a year to complete the design, prototyping, winning the order through the government tender process, and obtaining all the required certifications and approvals. We moved from Bengaluru to Delhi to set-up the factory in North India and fulfill the order. We had already stopped working on all our other projects for various IoT and automotive devices and products to focus on the smart meter as the order size was huge, and the govt has projected a huge demand. We didn't have any other product, customer, or revenue stream. We became bankrupt. When the first and second waves of Covid-19 were in full swing in Delhi, we did not have any emergency funds, and we were in the high-risk category due to comorbidities. All the state governments had started investing in health infrastructure, and they were not in a position to release any new tenders/orders for smart meters.

There are huge aspirations of lots of people attached to the product/project. It is necessary to have a survival mechanism in place. We must plan for situations where the funding stops, large orders get canceled, the vendor does not support warranty, natural calamities, pandemics, strikes, etc. We must work on our health as the top priority. Owner/ Partner should not be selfish to look at their personal interest alone. Thousands of employees, vendors, and customers suffered due to the misappropriation of funds in the Karvy Group.

C 2.6   Court Cases, Income Tax Department Notices, Bank's Calls

Startup owners face a lot of issues, and they may also find themselves in various litigations from vendor partners, customers, etc. There's a lot of pressure building from creditors, be it the bank or those in the market. Now, They endure the howling and yelling of the bank staff, who were once pleasant and kind when you held the status of their High Net Worth Individual (HNI) client with your corporate salary.

For court cases, founders have to travel across India to appear in court. The income tax department may open numerous cases, requiring you to respond with all the necessary documents within seven days, even for cases that are seven years old. Bouncers resembling recovery agents and lawyers visit the office, and threats become a norm. They have to bear the huge expenses of the lawyers. The travel time and expenses and the time taken for cases take a toll on their health. You are working hard to fulfill your dreams, and you will find yourself sitting with criminals in handcuffs, waiting for the judge to take up the case on the hearing date. This experience can disrupt your peace of mind, requiring efforts to return to the center and refocus on your business. Additionally, some big companies attempt to extract a lot from small organizations.

Ensure you consistently hire competent accountants, audit professionals, and lawyers after obtaining feedback from their previous clients or getting recommendations from someone trusted. Thoroughly vet all your work contracts with partners and stakeholders through your legal team to safeguard against unforeseen losses. Be mentally prepared for prolonged legal battles and resist fearing the police, judiciary and entire legal system, especially if you have not done anything wrong. Please proactively address any potential issues to maintain a strong foundation for your business success.

Your health and productivity would improve considerably without the endless sleepless nights caused by these cases.

We secured a loan against the property in which we resided; the only property we had left. One day, a bank official arrived unexpectedly to take pictures of the property. I remained oblivious of my organization's decision and was later informed by my accounts team that it was merely approval.

After a few days, the loan amount from the bank was in our accounts. It took me a couple of hours, perhaps minutes, to disburse the entire loan amount in clearing outstanding payments to vendors, partners, employees, etc, for which we committed to an EMI of Rs. 87000 per month for the next 30 years.

Managing calls from banks and ensuring timely payments during Covid-19 became challenging, leading us to eventually sell the property. Fortunately, we had transitioned to Delhi and were residing in my husband's grandmother's house in a posh society in Delhi.

C 2.7   Work for Govt for Volume

If you're looking for a volume that you cannot get from private sector customers, you must explore working for the government. The government order will not only provide you with a large order size and the pan India market, but it will also give you the immense satisfaction of contributing to the growth of India.

To secure a government order, you must showcase your capability, your previous order size, your revenue, etc. As a consortium of companies, We were supplying biometric attendance tablets, beacons, and smart energy meters to various state government and Central government offices. The government circulate tenders, organizes various events to attract investment, and awards MoU (Memorandum of Understanding) for collaboration. Government orders are difficult to win and have low profit margins, but they expose you to the large market and various other growth opportunities. The government orders are awarded after due diligence, and while the process may take time, they are entirely worth investing your time and money. You also need to make a lot of investment to supply and fulfill the order. Your payment will come to you at much later stages, but you can be 100% sure that your payment is secure, though it may get delayed due to various reasons. The other drawback is that the government asks for a long warranty, such as a seven-year warranty on the product at a very low cost. This is an additional financial burden on the manufacturer and the design house. You must look at maximizing profit from each client so you are not stuck grinding it out with razor-thin margins.

Mostly, the government requirements for devices, etc., are advertised through newspapers and awarded through a detailed and process-oriented tender process. They are mostly awarded to a reputable company, who meet the criteria specified by the govt. To meet the eligibility criteria, it is advisable to go as a consortium of companies to apply for any project. Before applying, make sure that the product meets all the specifications as per the government requirements and that all the certifications and approvals are in place.

If there were no government projects, we would have focused on supplying our home automation devices to various apartment buildings, large residential communities, hotels, etc. We would have supplied our various sensor-based devices and IoT devices to various business organizations and private companies, potentially at a higher profit margin. Such a strategy might have prevented us from bankruptcy caused by delays in receiving the payments from the government for the biometric attendance system.

Chapter 3

Startups or Corporate Jobs – To Plunge or Not To

"You never achieve real success unless you like what you are doing."

– Dale Carnegie, Self-Help Author

Some employees find the corporate job suffocating due to office politics, mundane work, fixed mandatory hours and limited growth. They believe that they will experience more growth in startups and decide to take the plunge. They must understand that entering into the startup world is a lifestyle change they and their families have to adopt. It involves a daily struggle to survive. They must weigh the pros and cons of leaving the corporate job and starting an entrepreneurship journey. In my experience, a combination of passion for your idea or product, coupled with patience and perseverance, has proven to be a key formula for success for startups.

Choosing between a startup and a corporate job involves weighing various factors with their distinct advantages and disadvantages. It's a decision that influences your potential for personal and career growth. However, among the commonly considered factors, individuals often overlook some aspects that may play a pivotal role in shaping a satisfying and fulfilling career path.

C 3.1 Renting Office Space and Hiring Talent

Having a good office space in a decent location is a necessity for any startup to convince the talent, the investors, and the stakeholders to associate with them. Besides pleasing the prospects, an office space provides discipline and a professional mindset to the founders and their employees. Rents for commercial spaces are huge. Founders are often compelled to compromise on building location, office size, and other facilities to meet their budget. At least in the beginning, a large part of the monthly expense goes into the rent for any startup. Hence, a lot of factors need to be considered before finalizing the office space.

Once you have refined your product or service idea and finalized the business plan, the next crucial step is securing suitable office space as per your requirements. Subsequently, consider designing elegant workspaces. If your budget permits, hiring an interior designer can help optimize the space to meet your requirements. Alternatively, You can-do the designing for cubicles, labs, and pantry areas yourself too. Any skilled carpenter will make the drawing and design as per your specifications. The carpenter will coordinate with the electrician and plumber in doing all the electrical fittings and civil work. Following this, purchase items such as comfortable chairs, state-of-the-art laptops, servers, software, test equipment, fridges, microwaves, cups saucers, cleaning supplies, stationery etc. From A to Z, ensure you procure all necessary items. Finally, the most important step of setting up the business is hiring technical staff, marketing and salespersons, finance folks, etc. For manufacturing, securing a spacious industrial area is imperative, usually located on the outskirts of the city, which may involve a significant commute for employees.

The process of finding an office space and setting up a full-fledged office requires the involvement of a real estate broker, interior designer, carpenter, painter, electrical and civil contractors, etc. The costs associated with each of these vendors are huge, and successful execution of the project demands a considerable amount of time. Founders need to have a lot of patience in the first few years of their business. Their initial investment lays the foundation for a conducive work environment, essential for the long-term success and growth of the business.

While on a corporate job, we take the state-of-the-art infrastructure of multinationals for granted; a dedicated team for infrastructure and facility management take care of everything. The employees are very much satisfied as they have access to everything.

C 3.2 Building Company Culture, Value Creation and Customer Delight

A strong, positive, vibrant, and high-performance culture is essential for an organization's success. Culture, strategy, and talent are the three main components responsible for long-term accomplishments. All three matter equally and are highly interdependent. When any one component is missing, the others lose their way.

The process of building company culture starts from day one. You must identify your values and place customer success as a top priority. Determine who you are and how you will behave even after you scale up. Having well-established work ethics and goals helps companies establish a strong foundation for their business. Scaling-up becomes an easier task as your employees, investors and customers trust you for your values.

Building the company culture starts with identifying your values and what you believe in. All your future actions and decisions will be governed by your values. It is important to identify the values correctly. The next step would be to create a vision and mission statement. Your vision will determine what you want to be, and your mission will determine how you want to go there. Learn your vision and mission statements by heart, live your vision and mission, and tell it to everyone you meet. Create strategies to meet the organization's objectives and vision. Work on the process, policies, and employee welfare schemes keeping in mind the vision of your company and the values of your company. Create an environment of authenticity and recognition where every employee feels appreciated, connected, and happy to contribute.

When establishing the company culture and adding value, it's crucial to comprehend the needs of stakeholders, understand government policies, and stay informed about new rules. Apply the lessons learned from your corporate experience. Document all policies, your vision, mission, and values. Share it with the employees and the other stakeholders through various communication channels.

In the absence of good company culture, the growth of the organization slows down. There are challenges in scaling-up. Employee satisfaction, customer satisfaction, and stakeholder satisfaction will be reduced.

C 3.3   Competition with Cheap Chinese Products

China has a strong manufacturing capability. Their production costs are very low compared to India. Being well-established as a global manufacturing hub they work on volume, which helps them control the cost while maintaining the quality.

China has a huge market worldwide for products based on semiconductor technology. Their infrastructure is massive, and the ecosystem is robust. They also have a strong support system from their government to boost manufacturing. In India, there is a significant duty on components that are imported. When we began, there were limited manufacturing capabilities for producing and assembling Printed Circuit Boards (PCBs). Optimizing the development time while maintaining the quality and cost in India was a major challenge.

After the prototyping stage, a few of our customers chose Chinese vendors to buy their ready-to-use products because it involved no additional development cost or development time. They could also decide the order size as per their consumers' demand and get minor customizations done to their product as per their requirements. The cost of prototyping done in India provided them with a strong data point for negotiation with the suppliers and all this made Chinese vendors very attractive.

If there were no Chinese products, we would have made products in India for our customers. That would have given a big boost to the Indian manufacturing sector and thus could have contributed to the economy of India. It would also have allowed huge customization options from the design stage as per the customer or market requirements. We would have succeeded much earlier.

C 3.4   Risk-Taking Appetite, Tight Deadlines and Pressure of Delivery

Startup founders have a huge appetite for risk-taking. Equipped with MBA degrees, their deep understanding of finance encourages them to start ambitious ventures, take big risks in the business, and invest a large portion of their personal wealth. And they are at an age, where they do not hesitate to experiment and take risks. However, the business environment imposes immense pressure due to tight deadlines and delivery commitments. Unfortunately, there is an industry practice to crush small vendors, organizations, and consultants. All these factors contribute to elevated stress levels and may lead to lifelong health issues.

Young startup founders make huge investments in the initial phase of their business without meticulously calculating the ROI. They have extensive knowledge but still need mentoring, guidance, and startup community and founder's forums support, etc., to manage efficiently in the volatile market and dynamic business scenarios. External reviews on products, pricing, processes, strategies, roadmap, and vision would help them receive feedback at the right time. Sometimes a lot of money from investors is put into the business without doing thorough market research, or product fit analysis. Investors too put a lot of pressure on profitability. They put their thought process and convictions that result in ego clashes between founders and investors.

We're living in the VUCA (Volatile, Uncertain, Complex, and Ambiguous) world. At times founders find it extremely hard to sustain in such an environment. They have to deal with pressure from all sides, customers, investors, vendors, employees, and families. Startups are not for the weak-hearted. You must develop a thick skin to survive in the startup scenario. You must work on your emotional intelligence. You also need to find a technique to channel out your anger, frustration, and pain so that your family, near and dear ones, and loved ones are not at the receiving end of your anger. Your employees also should not bear the brunt of your disappointments.

Some of these founders had amassed substantial personal wealth from their corporate careers. They accumulated assets through Employee Stock Option Plans (ESOPs) acquired early in their careers, along with dual incomes, and handsome salaries from their jobs. They do not hesitate to put their personal wealth into business. When their startup requires it, they quickly decide to liquidate their assets, sometimes facing disapproval from their families. This has financial and emotional repercussions for both founders and their families.

Without launching the startup, the founders may have experienced much more mental peace, work-life balance, and happier families. Many marriages suffer due to the prolonged stress the startup serves, partners become so engrossed in their business and life that they forget to laugh together, celebrate life, and enjoy simple things.

C 3.5 Coping with Changes and Crisis Management

Change is the only constant in our lives. Startup founders' lives are no different. To stay competitive in the market, they must continuously work on coping with our rapidly changing world and managing crises. They must embrace the changes, the greatest opportunities come from changes small or big, which lead to personal and professional growth while building resilience.

The change can occur from multiple sources such as customer requirement alterations, technology upgradation, team structure modification, marketplace changes, event changes, government policy/regulations revisions, etc. These changes can potentially lead to a detour in the startup's journey. Startup founders must be well-prepared to handle and manage these changes, as there are no firm guidelines on how to handle every situation. Founders need to rely on their experience, knowledge of the framework, proactiveness, and preventive actions to manage these changes without impacting the delivery and the relationship with stakeholders.

The future is never guaranteed in the startup world. There may be changes in the choices consumers make, market supply and demand conditions, and competitors' product and service landscape. There is nothing like stability in the startup world. Creating a change in your organization presents many possibilities. Whether creating change or responding to it, there are many opportunities for those who are open to adapting and embracing change. In the words of Helen Keller, "Often we look so long at the closed door that we do not see the one that has been opened for us."

If you are overwhelmed by fear and uncertainty of change, start by shifting your mindset. Acknowledge the changes, and understand that the possibilities are around the corner. Just like corporates, startups must have a contingency plan, a risk management plan, an escalation management plan, and a change management plan in advance. Founders and senior management need to devote a significant amount of their time to planning and brainstorming. Founders must update their employees, walk them through these plans, and assign responsibilities accordingly. In 9 -to- 5, there is ample support from senior management to create and implement these plans.

In situations where major changes are not required, the founders will focus mainly on the execution of the tasks required to fulfill their vision. They can prioritize marketing and sales and activities such as team building, networking, research, etc., for the growth of the organization.

C 3.6   Workplace Woes: Unproductive Meetings, Interpersonal Issues and Office Politics

The three biggest challenges most employees face in large organizations and corporates are interpersonal issues, unproductive lengthy meetings, and office politics. Those working in big corporates understand that people can be both the biggest support and the primary cause of stress. Contrary to common perception, the main challenges are not the work and deadlines but rather people's expectations, ego, fixed mindset, and attitude, which can make the 9 -to- 5 work-life bitter for many. In contrast, startup culture offers a less competitive environment, reduced cut-throat competition, and more growth opportunities.

In large corporates, employees find themselves in a constant cycle of proving their worth to secure their jobs, earn promotions, and stay in the good graces of their superiors. To maintain their positions, some may not hesitate to undermine others. Managers do not involve everyone in discussions. Most of the time, important decisions are taken during informal breaks such as smoke breaks, coffee breaks, etc. People who do not smoke and prefer to focus on completing their work and go home to take care of their families are left out; they are considered less serious, less career-oriented, and less responsible. The corporate culture is such that quiet workers are not appreciated. The thought leadership does not matter much. Gender bias issue still exists. Moreover, the long fixed mandatory working hours can be detrimental, killing creativity, productivity, and overall well-being. In contrast, startups are relatively smaller and more inclusive. The flat structure allows you to make decisions quickly.

In a job, long hours are often necessitated by tight deadlines and technical challenges. In projects, numerous participants are involved, and lengthy meetings are required to keep everyone informed and to reach a consensus before making decisions. These meetings also shape the plan and strategy for the project's course of action. However, it's important to note that lengthy meetings can also be counterproductive, wasting valuable time. The constant demand from customers for faster and more cost-effective solutions also adds to the pressure of deadlines. Additionally, teams may lack experience in implementing solutions, impacting project timelines.

Some individuals choose to work longer hours to socialize with friends and colleagues, often having meals in the cafeteria. They may also showcase higher responsibilities and workload by logging extended hours in the system to impress their bosses.

Corporates must encourage a friendlier environment and promote teamwork. This approach helps employees achieve a healthier work-life balance and stay focused on their tasks.

Their dedication, sincerity and better health will contribute toward the growth of the company. Fewer individuals will feel the urge to leave corporate life and start their own business.

C 3.7 Office Odyssey: Supportive Superiors, Challenging Clients and Connections

Managing interactions with colleagues, superiors, subordinates, clients, and other stakeholders can be an exciting and sometimes challenging journey. Support of bosses and super bosses in a corporate helps you develop the attitude and mindset of risk-taking, and exploring new solutions. It helps in dealing with demanding clients and adds valuable experience to your career growth. You also gain wisdom by working with difficult bosses and colleagues.

The corporate environment is designed to offer support for new mistakes, with bosses and systems assisting in handling clients with unreasonable demands and providing resources for firefighting. Protocols for escalation management are in place. In contrast, startups operate with limited budgets, time, and resources for projects, making the system less forgiving of mistakes. Startups often prioritize playing it safe to safeguard their reputation, clients, and finances. Layoffs due to employee mistakes are common in startups.

Corporate settings, on the other hand, may face issues arising from immediate managers, leading to stress caused by various factors such as communication breakdowns or ego clashes. Many employees opt to leave their positions due to conflicts with their managers and start their own firms to escape the challenges they faced. They aspire to become their own bosses and have control over their time, only to find themselves working around the clock, causing disruptions in their family life. Effective communication is essential. Employees should be encouraged to engage in healthy communication at all levels and through various channels. It's crucial to remind them that there is no such thing as over-communication.

Most employees and managers advocate for their teams and provide support so that they can work efficiently and grow in the organization. They create a learning environment and do not penalize the employees for their first-time mistakes. They encourage them to learn from failures. In return, teams reciprocate by delivering a high-quality solution, on time and within budget. However, It's essential to acknowledge that certain managers will sidetrack you. They will choose their favorites, and if they harbor any dislike, they may create hindrances in your promotion and overall growth. Disgruntled employees can tarnish the organization's image and destroy its culture.

Without the support of the bosses, employees feel demotivated. Their support and guidance provide them with the right opportunities, work-life balance and happy families. Happy families will create happy societies and in turn happy countries. Corporates have lots of support from the management and their HR department to take care of the well-being of employees. In startups, both founders and employees operate independently, creating a culture of autonomy and personal responsibility.

Chapter 4

Startup Satisfaction

"It's hard to beat a person who never gives up."

– Babe Ruth, baseball legend

Personal satisfaction is the most important ingredient for success. The life of a startup entrepreneur demands disciplined hard work. Through meaningful dedication and a sense of purpose in life, every achievement, whether small or large, tastes much sweeter. Founders believe in the beauty of their dreams; they are doers, and for them, success is a profound sense of fulfillment that satisfies their inner soul. The happiness found in creating something valuable and staying true to their dreams and values, makes the entrepreneurial journey worthwhile for founders.

C 4.1   Dream, Design and Deploy – Satisfaction of Creation

Every great product and discovery was an idea first, and the successful execution followed it. In the realm of product and service companies, the key approach is to dream, design, and deploy. Founders envision grand ideas, aiming for concepts that could potentially generate millions of dollars and distinguish them from others. Their focus lies in creating distinctive designs, that align with the needs of their customers. They undertake projects to develop products that meet specific requirements. Through careful attention to detail and a commitment to innovation, they strive to deliver products and solutions that not only meet expectations but also exceed them, contributing to a lasting impact in their respective industries. The journey from ideation to launch, from dream to deployment, brings immense satisfaction to those involved.

The product life cycle is long. The product has various stages from initiation to field support. Design, development, delivery, and deployment are different phases of the product life cycle. The journey is full of innovations and requires the implementation of technical, and logistical processes and resolution of interpersonal issues. The team is deeply invested in the project. Founders treat their products as their babies. They derive a sense of achievement in the creation of these products by closely following each of its phases, crossing every hurdle that they encounter and going into the next phase. When the product is successfully deployed the joy is boundless. After that, there's support in the field support and warranty assistance. Many people are drawn to startups for the sheer joy of creating something unique. This joy is incomparable to anything else. The passion, commitment, and dedication of the founders and team make the outcome more rewarding.

In the 9 -to- 5 job, you also have the same project lifecycle, but you may not be involved in all the aspects of the product's journey. As a startup founder, your involvement begins from the project's inception, where you have invested your blood and sweat. Family finds it difficult to understand, but startup founders are captivated by the satisfaction derived from the process. They forget all about their financial concerns and other worries by seeing the products in their hands and the services being used by end consumers.

Meticulous planning is required before the start and during the execution of the projects. Effective project management is the key to the success of any project. All the processes must be defined and followed for successful implementation. The project managers do not get their dues, but they play an important role in the success of the project. Founders must plan to have dedicated product and project managers for the successful execution of the projects. They are the right people who proactively identify and resolve all the issues. Some founders play the role of project manager and product manager, and they get involved in every activity related to project management and product development, while corporates have designated managers for these roles. The founder's involvement in project management impacts progress in other areas such as strategy, sales, etc. The project's delivery also gets impacted because of their on-and-off focus on the project.

Founders get disappointed when their products do not see deployment or success, and this failure results in consequences such as revenue loss, escalations, and customer issues. Resilient founders, despite facing these challenges, use setbacks as learning opportunities. They adapt strategies for future endeavors and persevere in their pursuit of long-term success.

C 4.2 New Market, New Product Initiation, Thought Leadership

Startup founders must continuously think through possibilities to develop and launch new, innovative, and impactful products.

They also need to explore new markets for all their products, existing and new. This will ensure that they are not overly reliant on a single offering or sector.

To successfully launch a new product and explore untapped markets, founders must conduct comprehensive market research, analyzing vertical, horizontal, and geographical segments. They need to decide on the target market, whether it's B2B (business to business), B2G (business to government), or B2C (business to customer). In-depth analysis of product-market fit, understanding customer requirements, and assessing end consumers' needs and market demand are crucial. Additionally, founders should consider competitive analysis to identify key players and potential challenges.

In any startup, a good knowledge of the market is vital. Thoughtful planning of the product's time to market and strategic positioning is essential to maximize profits and visibility, serving as the key to sustainability and survival in the startup world. Continuous monitoring of market trends and feedback from early adopters is equally important to adapt strategies and ensure ongoing success. Founders must also be agile and ready to iterate based on evolving market dynamics to stay ahead in the competitive business environment.

Founders must make efforts to stay abreast with the industry by reading the business news, learning through various other channels about the industry, and sharing informative content that addresses industry pain points and offers actionable solutions. Establishing yourself as a Thought Leader helps your tech startups attract investors, partners, and customers alike. It gives you a stronger competitive advantage and a market positioning. You are seen as an authority, a trusted adviser, a respected innovator, and a potential game changer.

Founders and their teams must also stay updated about changes in government policies, regulations, and directives. They also need to constantly stay in touch with their customers by talking to them about their requirements and consumers' expectations and taking feedback on existing products. They can then do analytical thinking and, to some extent, rely on their gut instincts before making any decision about the product and the new market. Balancing product development with market engagement is the key. Focus on sales and feedback from customers often leads to quicker adaptation and success. The feedback allows great products to steadily become exceptional. Do not make the mistake of building the best product in stealth mode; hoping that the 'best product' will sell itself can be a risky gamble. A missed chance in the market will not return. Build great products, but be a better marketer so the world can recognize your potential and the potential of your product. Startups should prioritize recruiting great marketers.

If founders do not incorporate the latest technology, their products will soon become obsolete. If they do not understand the demand in the market in the first place, they will lose on development costs for launching a product that is no longer needed.

If they are not talking to prospective clients, collecting pain points and solving their problems, they will not have a competitive edge or product-market fit. The team will be demoralized if they do not see the product successful. They will look for opportunities outside your organization. It will impact the credibility and reliability of the founders.

C 4.3 Live Your Vision, Mission and Purpose

Startup founders live their vision, mission, and purpose to achieve their goals. They also need to create a brand and an identity. They identify the values in which they believe and they conduct themselves. The process is very fulfilling and gives tremendous power to startup founders.

The vision describes what an organization aspires to be, where it wants to go, and what it wants to achieve over a 5-10-year span, outlining the overall direction. The mission articulates how the organization intends to reach those goals, providing a roadmap for the long-term. While the vision might evolve in five to ten years, the mission typically remains constant. Your purpose reflects your highest values and the positive impact you aspire to make. Founders must have a clear understanding of the vision, mission, and purpose, as this clarity facilitates the creation and implementation of strategies for organizational success and growth. Additionally, it aids in maintaining focus on the right priorities and creating consistency and discipline in actions. Sharing the vision, mission, and purpose with all employees is essential, and these guiding principles should always be visible to everyone within the organization.

The vision and mission must be documented and shared with all stakeholders, ensuring a clear understanding of what the company stands for and its purpose. Employees should consistently embody these principles, aligning all actions and behaviors with the organization's values. The organizational culture must be guided by these values to create a cohesive and purpose-driven environment.

If the vision, mission, and purpose of the organization are not defined, not communicated to all clients and employees, or not reflected in employees' behavior and the organization's culture, it will result in trust issues. The organization will lose its credibility. The brand name will be impacted. The company's growth will be stagnant, and the business will be unable to accomplish what it has set out to achieve.

C 4.4   Quality Control, Customer Success and Escalation Management

Quality control, customer success, and escalation management are key areas where a lot of time is spent by the founders. These factors also decide the success of the startup. Strict processes for quality control are required to launch the best product in the market. For founders, the motto is "customer success is your success", creating a win-win situation for everyone involved. Achieving repeat customers and ensuring customer delight are important success parameters. Founders collaborate with senior leadership from customers, vendors, and other stakeholders to effectively manage any escalations that may arise.

Startups must have a Quality Control Manager to ensure that all the test cases are captured and documented. Tests are executed. Test reports are duly filled in and shared with the customer and the internal teams. The internal and external review processes are followed at every step of the development. All this will ensure that there are no bugs found in the user acceptance testing performed by the customer.

Due to fund crunch, many founders also work as quality control managers. They want to launch the best product. To manage the escalations, the proper escalation plan must be laid out and must be followed. Communication is the key. Any delay, issues, or changes in the plan must be communicated to the customer.

The best way to ensure the product is being developed as per the specification and is of high-quality is by doing reviews at every stage and by creating awareness in the team about the importance of the work they're doing and how the quality of their piece of work will impact the overall product quality. Regular feedback should be taken from clients and senior management. Customers should be made aware that any delay in providing feedback or any other input will have an impact on the timeline and the quality of the product. Founders work hard to have the cost, schedule, and quality in control, resulting in happy customers and fewer issues and escalations.

The startups' success depends on their customers' success. Seek out customer feedback, listen to improve and work toward making the product better. Your most upset customers always have the best feedback.

The absence of quality control measures, customer management, and escalation management processes impacts the product quality, the organization's image, and customer relationships and ultimately results in loss of business and, in some cases, shutting down of the startup.

C 4.5   Learning from Failures

Founders will face failures. Failures provide necessary feedback. They must reflect on and learn from their failures so that mistakes are not repeated. Mistakes can sometimes prove to be costly. They must apply the learnings and realign the organization's goals and strategy with the vision of becoming a market leader.

The first step to learning from mistakes is to accept that there was a mistake and acknowledge the failure. Reflect on those mistakes. Do not move on before doing a deep analysis. Do not blame the team, brainstorm with them. Do not blame your luck, destiny, or timing, check your preparedness. Where were the inadequacies? Identify issues and resolutions, and immediately make a corrective plan and move to action. Update the team and stakeholders about changes in your strategies and the organization's objectives.

Document your learnings, the plan of action, and the issues and their resolutions. Review organizations' overall strategies, goals, and how they're aligned with the organization's vision. Are there any changes required in that? Review your product features. Is the product as per the customers' requirements? What changes can you make and deliver within the timeline agreed upon with the customer? Review your team's performance and figure out where they're lacking. Is there any training required? Are there any skills gaps? Identify the role or skill set that needs to be added to the team.

Mistakes are costly. If we do not learn from our mistakes the first time, we will make those mistakes again. Mostly, second-time mistakes do not allow us to sustain and survive in the startup world. Growth slows down, and the startup will need a much longer time to achieve growth.

C 4.6   Effective Leadership

Leadership plays a crucial role in a startup, shaping its vision, mission, and overall trajectory. Founders, as leaders, find immense satisfaction in creating the startup's brand, steering the startup toward sustained growth, and creating an impact in the industry. Be the leader your startup needs – always positive, believing, innovating and uplifting. If you don't believe, no one else will.

Leaders have a visionary outlook. They determine growth strategies and tirelessly work to realize the organization's vision. As role models, they inspire employees through engagement activities and offer leadership to stakeholders. They build strong customer relationships and their mere presence provides reassurance. Leaders play a pivotal role in overall industry growth by inspiring and collaborating with industry peers. They spearhead reforms and corrective actions, sharing valuable insights from their knowledge and experience at various industry forums. As they lead startups from struggle to success and through scaling-up phases, they mentor and groom future leaders along the way. They recognize that leadership is about the collective and know when to pass the baton. They chose their successor wisely.

Leaders need a mix of qualities to ace their responsibilities: discipline, dedication, and determination are the backbone. Having a clear purpose is a must. They should be approachable and tackle issues proactively. Authenticity and empathy make them relatable. Being bold decision-makers, they take swift action and shoulder full responsibility. Loyalty is their anchor, always aligning with the organization's vision. In essence, leaders are a powerhouse of traits that turn challenges into victories.

As a founder, focus on speed, culture, execution, vision, your story, team and brand – these are elements that set your startup apart and are challenging for others to copy. Resolve internal conflicts, encourage open communication, creative thinking and idea generation, and find ways to make your startup a fun workplace. Provide your team with everything they need to succeed.

Ineffective leadership impacts the entire organization. It creates dissatisfaction among employees, customers, investors, and other stakeholders. It greatly impacts the business and the quality of products and services delivered.

C 4.7   Continuity and Capacity Building

Founders must work on continuity and capacity building to stay current and competitive in the market and achieve long-term sustainability and success of the organization. This is required to build confidence in customers, employees, investors, and other stakeholders. This will also help you overcome any challenges and face unexpected events and changing circumstances. It will also help minimize downtime and financial losses.

For continuity and capability building, you must invest in enhancing technology and infrastructure, improving internal processes and strategies, constantly enhancing your product, and developing resources. Work with the latest technology, and machines, and continuously invest in research projects. Hire the best-in-class resources for the job. Create a culture of learning. Invest in training employees. Empower employees for skill-building. Understand what the customer wants. Simultaneously work on consulting projects to learn more about the industry and the latest trends. Make trends your friends. Invest your money and resources in research projects.

Founders must interact with industry leaders and work with technology companies. Take their reference design and develop a prototype. Study the industry trends, where the industry is heading, what innovations are there in the industry, and what new technology is being widely used in the field you are working on. Train your resources on the latest technology. Invest in skill-building of resources.

If the organization ignores these two important aspects, they will not be able to perform well, adapt to changing circumstances, and may have to shut down their operations. They may not compete with their competitors. If they were the market leaders, It would give an advantage to their competitors. Their most skilled and most loyal employees may not stay with them. They may join their competitors. It will hurt the founders the most.

We made it an ongoing practice to focus on both concepts. It helped us to overcome the following challenges:

1. We both had a decade and a half run in the software services industry; hardware design and product management were completely greenfield to us. Processors, Semiconductors, chips, PCB manufacturing and assembly, embedded systems, firmware, and BoM – were all foreign terms to us. There was also a dearth of skilled resources in the semiconductor industry but within one year, we were able to build a strong team consisting of industrial designers, mechanical designers, hardware engineers,

PCB designers, architects, firmware engineers and test engineers.

2. Over the span of a few years, we had an impressive product line of IOT devices, wearables, Bluetooth beacons, RF-based sensors, broadband devices like GPON, DVRs (digital video recorders), vehicle tracking system, digital identity and biometrics attendance systems, thermal printers and solutions in fintech space, Pigmy – Technology and solution for small savings. We even designed an Android phone running on Android Froyo (2.2) coupled with a 14 MP camera, unheard of in those days.

3. Many of our designs and solutions were ahead of their time. R&D efforts for new technologies at nascent stages need a lot of investment and patience to fructify. Venture funding for the hardware/manufacturing sector was hard to come by, and our vision of developing hardware capability for the country meant that we had to back our vision with personal money and endure financial hardship for years.

4. Product design is a long gestation game with a development life cycle, prototyping and test phase, marketing and mass production stages. Each of these requires large investments to make a successful product. Not every product will succeed commercially. The risk/reward ratio when we started back in 2011 was an uphill battle to fight.

5. There were very few opportunities to sell B2G devices with the government sector during the 2011-2015 period. B2C and retail opportunities for devices were crowded with cheap products from China.

Indian manufacturing could not match up to China then, neither in quality nor in cost.

6. We narrowed our focus then, to concentrate on B2B opportunities and started servicing and co-investing with partners that were bringing technology solutions to the Indian/Global markets that had a hardware/device component. We developed several GPON products including a one gig fiber box with 3X3 mimo WiFi capabilities for Reliance Jio, We also made the first working prototype for the Jio 4G mifi router. We made a wearable for Touchkin that could help manage old-age patient care. Several more devices were created for customers like Toshiba and many startups. However, none of these opportunities could give us volumes for production.

7. We hit our first big device order with Biometric attendance tablets in 2015. These tablets were to record fingerprint-based, Aadhaar-verified attendance of employees in Central government offices. We supplied and installed these tablets across India. Although driven strongly by the top leadership and the PMO, the device met with huge resistance from almost every government office. Officials resisted coming and leaving on time and damaged these devices regularly. We would then have to rush field service personnel to bring the device back to working status. The Aadhaar verification app was created and managed by NIC and would be down very often, creating logistical challenges. Most government departments delayed making payments to us, choking up our working capital. The purchase order from the government was on rather thin margins, and due to

these operational problems, we started incurring heavy losses. We had orders worth lakhs of devices but could finally supply only about 12,000. We kept supporting these devices for two years before giving up the business entirely.

8.   The worst tragedy hit us on 14th December 2015. Our CTO, a very respected and highly skilled leader in the hardware technology industry, was coming from his hometown, Chennai, to Bengaluru for work via state transport bus. Unfortunately, the bus met with an accident, and he tragically lost his life on the spot. He had always assured us that he would be with us until his last breath. He passed away at the age of 53. We were devastated but determined to realize his dreams.

9.   The partners that we supported couldn't bring device volumes to us. We then decided to create our own integrated solutions with apps and hardware components. With our experience of micro-lending, we created a fintech solution for Pygmy finance for rural banks and NBFCs integrated with an Aadhaar enabled thermal printer. We launched retail operations with this solution in October 2016 targeting collection agents and small shops that were offering services for the micro-lending sector. In November as Demonetization was rolled out, our retail operations were wiped out as the loan agents and shops stopped buying our equipment due to cash shortage.

10.   By 2017, we had seen losses in operations with the government, limited orders from B2B and our inadequate financial strength; there was almost no possibility of success with B2C devices either. With

financial strain mounting, we were bankrupt and almost ready to give up our dreams. However, we soldiered on with the belief that the longer we hang on, the more likelihood of success. We knew that hardware was a volume game, and the only way to hit it was to create a device that the government would purchase in large numbers. With the shrinking team, tottering finances, personal and family stress, and the toll on our health with years of hardship, we decided to create a smart energy meter design. Smart meters were projected to have a demand of 250+ million across India, with every household and every establishment getting it over the next 5-8 years. The worst of the crises brings the best of the opportunities, and amidst all the challenges, we could demonstrate our smart meter solution to the government and bag an order for five lakh devices with the condition that we need to finance the device supply.

11. We worked with the government of Rajasthan and designed and developed a tourism solution. Beacon devices were installed at various attractions in eight districts of Rajasthan to splash contextual information via our app onto tourists' mobile phones when they were in proximity of the specific beacon. The app also provided the user with live images of the attraction, its history, and information on various services nearby. Integration with aggregators for cab booking and PNR status checking was also done to provide a one-stop solution.

Chapter 5

Corporate Processes – Merits and Drawbacks

"The only way to do great work is to love what you do. If you haven't found it yet, keep looking. Don't settle. As with all matters of the heart, you'll know when you find it."

– Steve Jobs, Apple co-founder, visionary, entrepreneur

Corporates implement structured processes across various functions, including tasks such as employee onboarding, vendor invoicing, sales, customer service, accounting, asset management, travel coordination, performance appraisal, communication strategies, product development, project management, exit interviews, etc. Substantial investments of time and resources are dedicated to developing, automating, and optimizing these processes. The backbone of business growth and sustainability lies in effective process management. Well-organized processes not only help employees save valuable time but also elevate their productivity and contribute to a healthier work-life balance.

Despite these advantages, corporates must address potential drawbacks proactively and take measures to promote a more harmonious work environment. Supporting open communications and offering pathways for career growth can enhance employee satisfaction and loyalty, ultimately dissuading them from hastily venturing into their startups solely as an escape from corporate challenges. There are financial risks associated with entrepreneurship, as starting a business involves huge upfront costs and uncertainty. The challenges of building a client base and sustaining revenue streams pose additional hurdles. Moreover, the demanding nature of entrepreneurial endeavors can lead to increased stress for both founders and their families.

C 5.1   Global Delivery Model, 24*7 Support

The large companies working for global clients follow the Global Delivery Model GDM. The work happens almost around the clock, 24/7, from different locations. This is to increase the execution speed, take advantage of the different time zones, and support and maintain the production systems round the clock without having any downtime. Some people get the opportunity to work from the customer's locations and have proximity to the customer.

This model facilitates the equitable distribution of work across employees and locations so that no-one has to work odd hours and compromise on sleep. The work gets done fast. Communication is better between the customer and the team. There is no waste of time, effort, and energy due to miscommunication. It provides a better work-life balance for employees and customers. This enhances the customer satisfaction level and provides more reliable and stable systems for the customers and end users. With cost-effective offshore labor, the model capitalizes on network and infrastructure capabilities, enabling service delivery from any geographical location. Delightful customers, employees, and end users contribute to the growth of business for both customers and service providers.

The GDM requires a combined on-site and offshore presence to function effectively. In some instances, offshore workers may operate in two shifts. Teams are strategically positioned in both the service providers' and the customers' countries. Meetings and communication, facilitated through phone calls and video calls, occur during mutually convenient overlapping work hours.

Due to limited resources, both in terms of finances and personnel, a focus on the local market, and the complexities of overseeing remote teams, startup employees are unable to leverage the benefits of the GDM. The implementation of GDM in startups is also challenging due to rapid changes, adaptability and quick decision-making requirements, adjustment to evolving market conditions, and perceived risks and uncertainties in coordinating operations internationally. This hinders their capacity to tap into the advantages that a comprehensive GDM could otherwise offer in terms of efficiency, talent access, and market reach.

Without the implementation of a global delivery model, only 9 -to- 5 support will be available for critical systems. This limitation could lead to downtime during business hours, resulting in unstable systems, dissatisfied end users, and potential business loss for the customer. Additionally, it would increase development and maintenance costs for the customers.

C 5.2   **People, Processes, Product/Technology**

People, processes, and product/technology define an organization. They are the most valuable assets for the organization. They are the main contributing factors to the growth or failure of the organization.

Organizations must value these assets from day one. They must invest in state-of-the-art technology, training facilities, and the well-being of the employees. Startups must act like big corporates. They must focus on all these assets. If the growth slows down, the organization must look at the people, processes, and technology and see what is contributing to it. They must analyze it and act accordingly. The processes must be streamlined. They must be reviewed and revised as per the need. The technology must be up to date. Large corporates have learning departments that empower employees to work on their skill sets. The large corporates and their strong processes ensure that none of these assets become the cause for the failure of the project.

Large organizations take several steps to take care of their most valuable assets. Their leadership and project managers participate in defining the processes. Over time, their processes become robust; they are tried, tested, and revised multiple times. They hire the best-in-class talent. They give an environment of skill-building to all their employees. They invest hugely in the latest technology. The project teams working in an ideal environment produce high-quality products.

Startups often face multiple challenges, such as immediate survival concerns, pressure to scale quickly, talent retention issues, dynamic market conditions, and financial constraints, and they end up neglecting their most important assets.

If the organization does not have good people, processes, products, and technology, it will not be able to meet its vision and objectives. The growth slows down, they are not profitable, and they cannot be a respected company or the most attractive company for the stakeholders, and employees start quitting.

C 5.3   Set Processes and Strict Policies

Large corporates implement structured processes and stringent policies for their globally distributed workforce. This approach helps them to efficiently manage a vast employee base situated across various countries. These measures not only assist employees in effectively managing their time but also contribute to the overall enhancement of organizational profitability.

Rigid processes and strict policies without flexibility create problems for employees. It hampers their creativity and freedom to question, discourages risk-taking and critical thinking, and reduces time spent on research and experimentation. Employees blindly follow the process and feel dissatisfied and undervalued by the organization. They feel that their interests are not taken care of. They feel they will be penalized for making any decision outside the process boundary or policy guidelines. The managers also discourage their team members from taking any risks. Managers do not support their teammates when they make mistakes with any action taken without their approval. Employees feel stagnant. They do not feel they belong. They leave the organization at the first opportunity. Some may remain in their comfort zone by adhering to the processes and policies of the organization, which impacts their growth and the growth of the organization. It poorly impacts the organization's brand.

Corporates have their processes and policies documented. They are communicated to all the employees. Managers ensure that those guidelines are well implemented. There are systems in place to monitor adherence to these processes and policies. Employees are penalized if they deviate from the rules. The strict hierarchy and long approval processes delay decision-making, and a few frustrated employees take a plunge to start their organization.

Startups prioritize flexibility and provide a creative, innovative, collaborative and supportive environment. A positive work culture contributes to an individual's growth and helps startups attract and retain talent and succeed in the dynamic business environment.

Without processes and policies, there may be chaos. There will be no uniformity. Employees may find themselves spending more time on tasks, potentially impacting the clients. There will be no standard experience for customers as each project team will have their own processes. On the upside, creativity and risk-taking abilities may see an increase.

C 5.4   Average Appraisal Systems

Big organizations have fixed yearly appraisal systems to review performance, reward hard work, and recognize the exceptional contribution of the team members working on various projects.

The appraisal systems in big organizations often seem flawed. It does not focus on Key Performance Indicators (KPIs) alone set at the beginning of the appraisal cycle. Meeting KPIs with high quality alone is not sufficient for the bosses, they have a final say in the appraisal system. Employees on a bench with no project are also impacted by this process. They are compared to their peers actively working on projects. All the projects have different complexities, different sizes, different types of customers, technologies, and client-facing vs. delivery roles; all these factors are not taken into consideration during the appraisal process. Some companies even implement ranking within the mismatched group. Lower-ranked employees miss out on promotions and variable pay. While this may be justified for some due to their work ethics or skill inadequacies, sincere employees can feel disheartened, affecting their performance and overall team morale.

KPIs are discussed between the employees and the manager and are set in the appraisal system. These objectives must be achieved by the end of the appraisal cycle. After the cycle, employees are assessed based on their performance.

Organizations must make their appraisal system more employee-friendly and conducive to their career growth by implementing measures such as regular feedback, transparency and fair evaluation, 360-degree feedback., skill development opportunities, charting clear career progression paths, rewards and recognition framework and flexible appraisal methods. An effective appraisal system not only boosts individual growth but also strengthens the organization.

Without a structured system, employees may not work to their full potential and may have performance issues. The absence of comparison with fellow team members could promote the spirit of teamwork. Consequently, the organization will experience fewer disgruntled employees.

C 5.5   Certifications and Skill-Building

Staying true to Steve Jobs' advice, "stay hungry, stay foolish," corporates place great emphasis on skill-building. By upgrading their skills, employees experience a confidence boost and gain opportunities to work on projects using modern technology. Employers also attract and retain talent by providing a learning environment.

Big corporates have an extensive array of training options, including classroom, offsite, and online training, along with pre-recorded courses. They allocate a substantial budget to develop training infrastructure and make it obligatory for employees to complete a specific number of certifications annually. Mandatory training days are allocated for each employee. Corporates cover all costs, including international certifications, and foster a contagious learning environment where skill development is prioritized. Certifications and skill-building efforts directly influence employee performance in the appraisal system. Collaborations with universities and online academies grant employees free access to a wide range of courses, contributing to their overall growth. This not only transforms the organization's culture but also enhances its brand image, turning employees into lifelong learners who, in turn, significantly contribute to the organization's growth.

Project managers, in their project plans, make provisions for mandatory training days for all the team members. These are not billed to the customer. Project managers also calculate and showcase the tangible benefits of training on parameters such as productivity improvement, reduced number of defects, etc., to the client and their senior management. This further encourages employees to invest time in skill-building and employers to increase their training budget.

In the startup culture, emphasis is often placed on agility and adaptability, and employees are encouraged to learn on the go. The resource constraints and evolving priorities of startups may lead them to prioritize informal, just-in-time learning over formally allocated training days.

Employees may experience a sense of stagnation in the absence of skill-building and training activities. Their untapped energy will not be channeled properly, and they may also have to face layoffs.

C 5.6   Inequality, Gender Parity and Lack of Clarity in Career Design

Corporates celebrate diversity as the driving force behind innovation and success in the organization. Equality is not just a corporate responsibility but a collective journey toward a brighter, fairer future. Selfish managers, cut-throat competition, continuous stress to meet the expectations of clients and bosses, and pressure from senior management are the primary reasons for gender inequality and lack of clarity in career design.

Many corporates lack assigned mentors for employees, seeking career guidance, leading to confusion amid frequent rotations within and outside business units. Ambiguous promotion guidelines and favoritism from managers create disparities, with some leaders sidelining women. Women face challenges as organizations favor a hustle culture, equating leaving on time with being less career-oriented. To counter this perception, women often work extra hours. Seeking solace in shared struggles, women tend to bond and form support systems. Additionally, strict anti-sexual harassment guidelines sometimes deter close working relationships between genders to prevent potential issues arising from miscommunications or perceived inappropriate behavior.

Organizations support a hustle culture where planning meticulously and working efficiently is not sufficient, where working long hours, caffeine-fueled late nights, and putting out last-minute fires are considered hard work, and where putting things off until they require a heroic effort to complete on time are rewarded. There are a few cases where long hours are appropriate, but organizations must work on creating a culture of sustainability.

Startups promote a collaborative environment where open discussions about career paths are encouraged, and everyone's contribution is acknowledged. The absence of rigid hierarchies in startups also gives a sense of equality, making it a more dynamic and inclusive space for all employees.

The culture of equity will provide equal growth outcomes for everyone, and accepting different perspectives from employees in key decisions will make every project a great success and an organization a great place to work.

C 5.7 Working Across Domains, Geographies and Technologies

Large corporates operate globally, providing their employees with opportunities to travel and work at various customer locations worldwide. This exposure not only introduces them to diverse cultures and work environments but also exposes them to new technologies, roles, and new learnings, promoting professional growth and developing a broader skill set.

Due to the expansive customer base, employees at the corporate level are presented with opportunities to work on different domains and technologies for various clients. This allows them to identify their niche in domain and technology through diverse projects. Even in cases where they find themselves in the wrong role or working with the wrong technology, there is often an option for rotation within or outside the business unit. This exposure provides them with opportunities to meet new people and acquire new skills while staying relevant in the market by working on cutting-edge technologies.

In situations where individuals encounter challenges within their team, experience irreparable differences with their bosses, or need to relocate due to personal reasons, corporate employees often have the flexibility to explore alternatives. Corporates generally have policies that support employees' needs, contingent on alignment with client agreements without any impact on business operations. Conversely, startup employees may lack these benefits and feel constrained in their roles at times.

Within large corporates, employees have the flexibility to transition across domains, technology stacks, roles, cities, and countries through internal job postings, promotions, references, direct contacts, etc. There are policies in place to facilitate these rotations, catering to the personal and professional needs of employees and contributing to the overall satisfaction of both employees and their families. This supportive environment enables employees to concentrate on their work, promoting growth for both themselves and the organization.

Without the flexibility to choose domains, technologies, and locations based on employees' interests and needs, they would experience limited exposure, reduced employability, and might remain within their comfort zone. The comfort zone poses risks for both employees and employers.

Chapter 6

Startup Learnings

"To me, business isn't about wearing suits or pleasing stockholders. It's about being true to yourself and your ideas and focusing on the essentials."

– Sir Richard Branson, Entrepreneur, Virgin Group Founder

Building a successful organization from the ground up requires vision, dedication, perseverance, strategic thinking, meticulous planning, and effective execution. The journey of a startup founder is often lonely. It is marked by numerous hurdles and challenges, each contributing to unique lessons and stories and the satisfaction and pride of having overcome them.

Enjoy the startup journey without stressing too much about the end goal. Instead of just caring about numbers, give your best, generate creative ideas, add value and make a difference. Aim for fulfillment, not just fame, and seek satisfaction, not just recognition. If the beginning is tough, don't give up; persist, endure, and establish your brand. The key is to keep going and stay consistent for startup success! Adaptability is advantageous; always be open to change and learn along the way. Surround yourself with a supportive network, as collaboration often leads to greater progress and innovation.

Don't shy away from challenges; view them as opportunities for growth. Welcome feedback, value constructive criticism and continuously refine your approach. Make resilience your main source of energy for your startup journey. Keep in mind that steady effort and persistent commitment lead to long-term success in the shining startup world.

C 6.1   Health is Wealth – Physical and Mental Well-Being

Prioritize your well-being because good health is the foundation of success. Without a healthy body and mind, achieving success becomes challenging. Physical and mental well-being brings clarity and enables one to give the right energy and focus where needed. Always remember the equation:

Success = Health + Happiness.

Good health provides numerous benefits for startup founders. Health gives discipline, mental clarity, agility, and improved decision-making. It makes you a role model, earning the trust of stakeholders. It helps founders manage their time and energy efficiently and enhance their productivity. It brings about emotional stability that helps manage work-life balance and relationships. A healthy foundation enables business expansion, positive and productive workspaces and rapid growth.

Startup founders focus on multiple critical areas amidst pressure from investors, clients, vendors, employees, family, etc. They should dedicate a "golden hour" each morning to physical and mental health. They may include 20 minutes for exercise and sunshine, 20 minutes for meditation and affirmations, and 20 minutes for reading and journaling. In the night, they should reflect on the day, identify the golden moments of the day, and plan for the next day.

Giving the highest value to fitness is the first step to achieving good health. Planning and setting your health goals, eating nutritious food, exercising regularly, meditating, getting good quality sleep of 7 to 8 hours most days, and making simple lifestyle changes can go a long way. With a healthy body and mind, you can always get back to winning and growing; you can lose it all and rise back. Your health is the most important aspect to take care of, as it plays a crucial role in your performance.

Poor health can lead to lethargy, procrastination, and the risk of missing important milestones. These outcomes hinder the founder's ability to lead effectively, make sound decisions, and manage the complexities of running a startup. Additionally, it may adversely impact relationships with stakeholders, employees, and even personal networks, potentially eroding trust and confidence. Overall, the result of poor health among founders can create a domino effect, impeding the growth and success of the startup.

C 6.2 Pursue your Passion for Mental Strength

Passion is the fuel for mental strength – the more you pursue it, the stronger your mind becomes. Engaging in your passion is an excellent stress reliever, lifting your spirits and boosting confidence immensely. With newfound confidence, you can accomplish greater things in all aspects of life. This is particularly crucial for entrepreneurs, as embracing their passion offers a unique source of inspiration and innovation, which can be instrumental in overcoming challenges and driving business success.

You can follow your passions alone or find mentors to guide you; mentors are the best advisers. The right mentor helps you discover your true abilities. Try new hobbies or pick up old ones and spend some time on them every week. This connection with your interests boosts creativity and gives you the mental strength to grow in all areas of life. It also improves your problem-solving skills, making it easier to handle challenges at work. Engaging in your hobbies helps manage negative emotions like anger and stress and creates harmony in relationships.

Join communities with people who share your interests, attend live classes, and soak in the group's energy to achieve your personal and professional goals. Open up new possibilities; there's no limit to what you can achieve.

A vast array of skills and hobby courses are accessible on YouTube, and there are also dedicated online academies where you can purchase courses or join live classes. Consistent practice is the key; not only does it enable you to learn a new skill or enhance an existing one, but it also contributes to improved concentration on your work and the successful attainment of your goals.

Neglecting our passions can turn life into a monotonous routine, solely revolving around work. Without actively pursuing what we love, personal growth stagnates, and our true potential remains untapped. Embracing our passions is essential for a more fulfilling and meaningful life. It enhances creativity, gives us a purpose and develops a well-rounded perspective.

C 6.3   Empowering a Vision and Purpose Larger Than Life

We must have a vision and purpose that surpasses conventional aspirations, and strive for the holistic welfare of our employees, clients, and stakeholders. This overarching vision is vital for the greater good of our community, the advancement of our country, and addressing global challenges with innovative solutions.

Evolve an expansive vision and have strong belief and confidence in its realization. Develop innovative solutions to address your customers' challenges, always keeping a broader perspective in mind. Nurture a desire to contribute meaningfully to your country by establishing a legacy, generating employment, and actively participating in economic growth. Develop an environment for the emergence of leaders, for true greatness lies in creating others who excel. Give back to society by serving with kindness and compassion to people around you.

Build capabilities and aim for excellence. Your vision and purpose will guide your actions and motivate you daily. They will inspire good habits, efficient time management, and a focus on your physical and mental well-being. With these, you will put in more energy and enthusiasm to achieve your goals, find more creative solutions to problems and overcome any obstacles in your way. Your vision and purpose make you unstoppable; they help you create a lasting impact.

Keep working toward your goals in line with your vision and purpose. Remind yourself and those around you about your vision and purpose regularly. Stay dedicated to your objectives and understand the reasons behind your actions. Don't be swayed by external opinions, as not everyone will understand your purpose. Keep your team, loved ones, and acquaintances informed about your vision and purpose. Teams are more engaged and confident when they know the organization's direction and strategies. Conduct your business with the utmost integrity and secure your position as a responsible and respected leader in the business world.

Without a vision and purpose that extends beyond the ordinary, our progress will be limited, and our reach will remain confined. With a narrow focus on self-interest, we risk staying small and will miss out on creating an impact.

C 6.4 Achieving Excellence Through Targeted Efforts, Simplicity, Small Triumphs

In the pursuit of success, founders must remember that it's not about the multitude of paths but the steadfast commitment to the chosen one. Small wins are the milestones that lay the foundation of monumental success. Maintaining a focused approach and acknowledging small wins are crucial for founders. This not only keeps them on track but also serves as motivation to work toward the organization's objectives with impact. Such a mindset is essential to avoid falling into the trap of the "shiny object syndrome", which can divert attention and resources from the core goals and hinder long-term success.

In today's complex business environment, simplicity is often overlooked, leading to unnecessary complications.

Yet, there is inherent beauty in simplicity, and it is crucial to recognize its power. Celebrating each milestone, no matter how modest, boosts team morale. Clearly defined goals and a comprehensive understanding of our identity and objectives enable focused efforts, ultimately saving time. Enlightening the team about the impact of simplicity, maintaining focus, and cherishing small victories energizes them, significantly boosting productivity and steering the company in a positive direction.

To succeed, it's important to have clearly defined objectives and goals. Have clear, crisp, regular communication with the team. Prioritize tasks wisely and know when to decline additional responsibilities. When necessary, pivot with purpose in alignment with core values and long-term objectives.

Lack of focus leads to working on multiple things and spreading attention across various objectives. This complicates the journey, confusing both customers and stakeholders. None of the goals will be accomplished because of this, and the team will be demoralized.

C 6.5   Unleashing Success Through Persistence, Discipline, Hard Work and Family Support

In the pursuit of startup success, there are no shortcuts; hard work, persistence, and discipline are the keys to building confidence, overcoming challenges, and achieving your entrepreneurial goals.

Achieving success in any profession, organization, or business demands dedicated hard work. For startup founders, weekends often become a luxury they can't afford. Socializing, spending time with family, and taking vacations gradually fade away as they immerse themselves in chasing their dreams. It's crucial to involve families in this journey, keeping them informed about the organization's progress and challenges.

Founders maintain constant accessibility to employees, clients, and other stakeholders and family and friends, essentially becoming superheroes who bear the brunt of stress alone, shielding their teams and families. Founders often have to make tough decisions alone, hence few know the reason behind the path they have taken. The unrelenting work, absence of breaks, loneliness, and enduring stress inevitably take a toll on the founder's physical and mental well-being. Understanding, patience and unconditional support from family members help them cope with the ups and downs.

Family support is crucial, and apart from sharing achievements, it's important to communicate the current challenges effectively. This includes detailing the organization's roadmap, potential financial challenges and their impact on personal life, existing liabilities, and loans while also exploring possible solutions. Engaging the family in understanding these challenges and seeking their advice is essential. In Indian families, bonding often revolves around food and enjoyable discussions, with politics taking center stage, but personal and financial problems are seldom addressed openly.

When stakeholders observe a lack of persistence and discipline in the founders' efforts, it breeds insecurity and forms a negative perception of them. This unfavorable image has repercussions on the organization, its employees, and their families.

C 6.6   Think About Only Things in Your Control

"You have power over your mind – not outside events. Realize this, and you will find strength."

**– Marcus Aurelius, Roman Emperor,
Stoic philosopher**

Focus on what matters and what you can influence. You won't get any results by thinking and worrying about things that are not in your control. It drains your precious energy and deviates you from the path to success.

To succeed, set clear goals and avoid overthinking. Overthinking will stop us from fulfilling our duties diligently. It is imperative to have a detailed project plan, a risk management strategy, a resource allocation dashboard, a well-structured schedule, regular progress reviews, and consistent updates to the team, clients, and stakeholders. Some situations and circumstances will always remain beyond our control. We cannot control other people's opinions, actions, feelings, and behaviors. We cannot govern the market or the emergence of new government policies, regulations, or restrictions. What we can control is our attitude and mindset, which, when positive, enable us to work with full focus. It requires us to prioritize the health of both our body and mind and learn to concentrate even in a disruptive environment. It leads to greater clarity, an important trait for leaders.

Eliminating unproductive tasks to free up more time for valuable work is essential. Using Stephen Covey's time management matrix, we can identify and prioritize important tasks and give our best efforts. Taking responsibility for actions within our control provides a sense of empowerment.

For instance, if job applications and interview preparation don't yield any calls, rather than stressing, take proactive steps to maintain optimal health.

Avoid overthinking by planning your day well, empowering yourself, and making yourself resourceful. Overthinking can result in low productivity, increased stress, poor outcomes, and missed targets. It hinders your ability to make prompt decisions and take swift actions. The cost of overthinking is huge.

Productivity, profit, promotions, performance, and professional and personal growth matter, but life isn't just about output; it's also about finding passion and purpose, being creative, and building relationships. Focus on what brings joy, and fulfillment and makes a positive impact on the world around you instead of just doing more and making more.

C 6.7 Crafting a Vision Board for Clarity, Direction, Inspiration and Success

Make a vision board—it's like a magical map that makes you dream big and move toward a fulfilling future. This will align your dreams with actionable steps. This will give you daily reminders and illuminate your path to work toward your goals. The practice is followed by almost all top performers and it works because it gives them courage and makes them take action.

Craft a vision board covering all aspects of your life – business, health, wealth, personal growth, relationships, etc. Envision your desired state, set ambitious goals, and dream big. Ask yourself key questions – Who do you want to be?

What kind of person would you want to become to feel proud of yourself? What do you enjoy doing? What are your ultimate goals? Find the answers, and bring your dreams to life on your vision board. Keep it in view, take action, and witness positive lifestyle changes. Make it a habit to think positively, align your vision with actions to propel you toward your goals, and experience exponential growth in every facet of your life.

Direct your attention toward personal and business growth, flourishing health and wealth, and harmonious relationships. Your focus determines your reality. Train your subconscious mind to create a positive self-image and have a strong belief in your deservingness of success and abundance.

Without a vision board, your aspirations diminish, reducing your chances of achieving greatness. Life may become mundane without this powerful tool to guide and inspire you.

C 6.8   Multitasking is Outdated

Multitasking often produces lower-quality outcomes as humans are inherently incapable and quite inefficient when it comes to doing two things at the same time. Additionally, with multitasking, the likelihood of making mistakes rises, which results in increased stress, inefficiency, and extended completion time.

Some individuals believe that multitasking is a time-saving skill, thinking they can efficiently handle multiple tasks simultaneously. However, this approach often leads to short-term productivity, followed by increased stress, elevated blood pressure, fatigue, and strained relationships. Blaming others may follow. Multitasking generally results in subpar performance across the board. It's beneficial to focus on a single task for as long as possible. In startup environments with a small team, it's advisable to concentrate on two or three products, ensuring thorough attention throughout the development, marketing, sales, launch, and support phases. Once these products attain success or a certain market presence, then consideration for additional products can commence. Similarly, at home, it's beneficial to dedicate time to specific activities, like eating and then watching television. It will be easier as you will recognize, realize, respect, and relish what you are eating, and you will rejoice with family members. It creates a deeper appreciation for each experience and enhances family connection.

Multitasking becomes necessary when tasks are not adequately planned or prioritized. Founders frequently find themselves multitasking, driven by overconfidence in their own abilities and a lack of confidence in delegating tasks. This can lead to burnout and decreased overall productivity. However, by creating effective time management strategies, preparing a project plan, and building a reliable team, entrepreneurs can reduce the necessity for constant multitasking. This, in turn, leads to a more sustainable and successful entrepreneurial journey.

By refraining from multitasking, each task is approached with mindfulness and undivided attention. This approach allows for a heightened appreciation of the activity, enabling a thorough understanding of its purpose. Consequently, we gain the ability to identify optimal methods for automation or task accomplishment. This dedicated focus contributes to the production of high-quality products, increasing the likelihood of their success in the market.

Chapter 7

Allahabad to Bangalore: From Ganges to Garden City

"Life is a series of natural and spontaneous changes. Don't resist them – that only creates sorrow. Let reality be reality. Let things flow naturally forward in whatever way they like."

– Lao Tzu, an ancient Chinese philosopher

When we leave our hometown for a new city to work, it's like spreading our wings into the unknown skies of opportunities. We take a courageous stride toward personal and professional growth facing the challenges and new possibilities that lie ahead in unfamiliar territories. The journey reveals to us a broad spectrum of experiences, diverse cultures, and fresh relationships. It makes us adaptable, stronger, and flexible, shaping us into more independent, and versatile individuals. We also discover our inner strengths and develop a sense of self-reliance that stays with us throughout our life's journey.

C 7.1 Scholastic Success: Ranking 1ˢᵗ in Class, Entering MNNIT

Childhood embodies innocence, and I, too, was an intelligent and innocent child. Even today, I receive compliments for retaining my innocence and childlike qualities. Jealousy and comparisons were foreign concepts to me.

My childhood was a blessing, rooted in the blend of tradition and progressiveness within my family. Education held a paramount place, giving me and my siblings, confidence and courage. I exhibited early signs of independence, steering my sister's Luna moped through the neighborhood streets even before learning to cycle. Diwali, with its crackling crackers and cheerful celebrations, was a cherished festival, and my fearless enthusiasm for fireworks never waned.

With a perpetual smile and a can-do attitude, I lived a disciplined life. Studying was the passion, I shared with my four sisters, and after finishing my academic pursuits, spending time with Daadi, Mummy, and my siblings was my favorite pastime. My father, dedicatedly managing his wholesale shop specializing in locks and related items, forged a strong bond with my mother and all of us. Through my parents, I learned that it takes effort and commitment to establish strong bonds that become inseparable over time. In our joint family, uncles, aunts, and cousins created a protective and fun-filled environment.

Born into a business-class family with the societal expectation of a male heir, my parents defied stereotypes, They never made us feel that we were any less. Determined to excel academically, two of my elder sisters pursued MBBS from Allahabad Medical College, and I joined the National Institute of Technology in Allahabad.

Encouraged by supportive parents and inspired by my sisters, I delved into my passion for mathematics. Consistently securing the top position in my class, I recently learned that some parents inquired about my examination answer sheets, curious about my consistent academic success.

If not for engineering, I envisioned pursuing a PhD in Mathematics and leading a simple and stable life in a small town.

When my startup faced challenges, I started considering returning to corporate life for the sake of my family. Despite encountering obstacles and rejections in the job market, I remained resilient. Request for friends' referrals got a cold response. It was a stark reminder that everyone appears smart when in a position of power. Drawing strength and confidence from past successes when tackling new challenges always helps.

C 7.2 Adapting: Moving from an All-Girls School to a Co-Ed Class With Three Girls

Upon entering the engineering college, the environment changed completely. Having studied in a girls-only school and staying at home with all my sisters, I suddenly found myself in an environment dominated by men. However, I discovered that a co-ed environment encourages greater understanding, increased interaction, more interesting classroom discussions, and different perspectives.

Most engineering colleges had a very poor gender ratio in the 1990s. There were 23 girls in the class of 300, and in the electrical engineering class, we were only three girls among 60 boys. In those days most girls preferred to take biology or arts subjects; jobs after engineering were associated with working on the shop floor in factories.

Accustomed to a sheltered family environment where my bond with my mother was strong, the transition was a bit challenging, especially due to the poor implementation of anti-ragging steps. Given the distance from home and the secluded surroundings of my college, I opted to stay in the hostel. Situated in a village area, the college surroundings were serene, but hostel security was stringent, enforcing strict timings. Interactions with male peers were limited, and surprises like mass bunking plans by boys often caught us off guard. Our trio, along with the professor, would occasionally turn up to a lecture hall expecting a full class, only to find it surprisingly quiet. A reserved front bench became our designated space.

During a recent reunion, I took the opportunity to reconnect with my classmates whom I hadn't known well during college. Despite the limited interaction with the broader student body, I formed a close-knit group of friends, and our outings and visits to college cafeterias, movies, and city centers were cherished moments.

The social culture of UP was different from that of other states. When I landed a job in Karnataka, my parents were happy that I left behind a non-progressive state. My outlook changed completely when I moved to Karnataka. The situation in these two states is different now.

The inclusive approach enriches our educational journey and equips us with essential life skills such as empathy, adaptability, teamwork, interpersonal skills etc required for personal and professional growth.

C 7.3   Relocating Roots: Allahabad Bids Adieu, Bangalore Beckons

I got selected by Siemens, India during college placement, fulfilling my dream as an electrical engineer. After successfully clearing multiple rounds of interviews, including those in Delhi, and undergoing thorough medical checkups, the official joining date remained pending. As the recruitment cycle was concluding, Hindustan Aeronautics Limited (HAL) extended a placement offer, and I felt glad and appreciative to accept it. The initial training for all recruits was scheduled in Bangalore.

On my travel to Bangalore via Chennai on the Ganga Kaveri Train, my parents and a younger sister accompanied me, and we stayed at a family friend's daughter's place in Chennai. She was newly married, and we were grateful for the warmth and hospitality extended by her new family. This marked my first visit to a South Indian city and my initial experience of the beach, a sight previously only seen in Bollywood movies. The journey marked the beginning of several memorable firsts.

Upon reaching Bangalore after two days, I celebrated my 22nd birthday at HAL Staff College, with the formal joining scheduled for the following day. The staff college and participation in residential management training courses provided a valuable learning experience. Landing in Bangalore, I instantly fell in love with the city's charm and delightful weather. I had my first South Indian Thali meal with my parents at Kamat in Majestic. My father was curious to try local food. He was slightly upset when I could not relish that meal. It took me around a year and a half to start appreciating South Indian food.

Despite occasional pangs of homesickness, I cherished everything else about the city, often recounting the pride of meeting Rakesh Sharma, the first Indian astronaut who ventured into space and testing Automatic Flight Control Systems for Advance Light Helicopters. Bengaluru offered a refreshing contrast with no instances of eve teasing or the sweltering heat. Although I missed home at times, my friend from IT BHU, now at Infosys, frequently visited me at HAL. I also formed meaningful friendships during my time at HAL.

Reflecting on this, I recognize that if I hadn't embraced the opportunity to move to Bangalore, I would have remained in my home state, leading a simple, small-town life and foregoing many incredible experiences.

C 7.4   Daily Jaunts from HAL Hub to the Magical Charm of MG Road

My friend PP and I got to know each other through a mutual friend in IT BHU. We had met 4-5 times in Allahabad, and during our engineering days, we became pen friends. His letters were filled with humor, and not just me, but all my hostel friends enjoyed reading his witty notes. The weather in Bangalore, especially for someone accustomed to the scorching summers of North India, was unimaginably beautiful.

PP used to commute daily from Jayanagar to Electronics City, taking the company bus in the morning and returning in the evening. He would then ride his bike from Jayanagar to HAL. Back then, with no Inner Ring Road, the route through Vellara Junction was quite long. We made it a routine to visit MG Road and Brigade Road almost every day, something unimaginable now: one must take a full day's holiday from work to do this trip alone in present-day Bengaluru. It marked a newfound financial freedom for both of us.

MG Road held a magical charm, and I thoroughly enjoyed every aspect of my personal and work life. The residential management training program was exceptional, featuring guest teachers from various management institutes.

Coming from a business-class family, where I used to count cash collected at the shop daily, the transition to receiving a monthly salary was initially challenging, creating a sense of discomfort. This brought a newfound respect for businessmen, especially my father, whose hard work and dedication were truly incredible. He never complained about long working hours or hardly taking holidays. Our home had an abundance of everything. I spent almost all of my first salary in a day buying presents. In a thoughtful gesture, PP used a part of his first salary to gift me beautiful heart-shaped gold-plated earrings from Mota Arcade. I will always cherish this gesture.

In September, Siemens called me to Delhi, and I boarded my first flight from the old HAL airport in Bangalore to Delhi. I vividly recall the ticket price of 6300/-, which exceeded my first salary. Although I reached Delhi, my heart was set on the life I had grown to love in Bangalore.

With PP, I explored the streets of Bangalore. During VIP movements at the airport, we would take alternative muddy roads, and on one occasion, we experienced a bike fall on such a road. On days when PP couldn't join in the evenings, I played badminton at the staff college with my HAL friends and enjoyed canteen food. PP experienced an accident with a car at one point. So, after completing my training, I chose not to opt for the HAL staff quarter and instead moved to a Paying Guest (PG) accomodation near PP's rented place. It was a luxurious house, and I enjoyed staying with my delightful landlady Mrs Anita Malhotra in a family-like environment.

C 7.5   Across Continents: A Tale of Living in the USA and UK

In Bangalore, much like everyone else, I got fascinated with the IT industry – its work, offices, unique work cultures, the luxury of a two-day weekend, etc. One day, while at the HAL office, I noticed a walk-in interview advertisement for IBM, located approximately 1 km away from my office. Intrigued, I decided to attend and successfully cleared the written exam and subsequent interview. When I returned home that evening, my landlady shared the exciting news that I had been selected. She had received the call on the landline.

Being on probation at HAL, my father provided the necessary funds for the Rs 25000 bond amount, marking my transition from one corporate giant to another. At IBM, I formed numerous friendships, and my career took me on my inaugural international trip—a short-term assignment in Texas, USA. Coincidentally, PP was in California, adding to my joy in reaching the United States. Upon completing his assignment, PP informed me during his return flight that he had purchased a ring for me. With my parents and family visiting his hometown for the roka ceremony, I saw this as the perfect opportunity for engagement. After discussing the matter with my boss and the customer, I promptly boarded the next flight to India, where we were engaged. Fast forward 25 years, and our journey continues.

After a delightful courtship of 8 months, we embarked on the journey of marriage. Anticipation filled the air as I eagerly looked forward to the upcoming union. In Punjabi traditions, the first year of marriage holds special significance, marked by vibrant celebrations of festivals with the extended family. With a desire to be in India and experience the joy of every festival, we secured a lovely, independent residence in the upscale locality of Koramangala before our wedding. Leading up to the grand occasion, we made several household items purchases, including a new car, fridge, washing machine, TV, bed, and more. These preparations culminated in our destination wedding in the holy town of Pushkar, an event that remains a cherished memory for both our families to this day.

On our wedding day, the caretaker at home shared the news of a call from the office. PP, elated, assumed it was his business manager calling to extend congratulations on our wedding. The following day, excitement turned to surprise when he revealed that his interview with a major US client was scheduled for that night. This project, involving a large bank venturing into outsourcing, had faced two rejections before. PP, succeeding in the interview, was asked to join immediately. Our honeymoon plans to Singapore and a cruise to Thailand were canceled abruptly, despite the tickets and visas being ready. PP swiftly collected his documents and headed to the US. Meanwhile, I stayed back, overseeing the sale of our possessions—TV, fridge, washing machine, car, etc.—and vacating the house. On that day, I decided not to harbor any love or attachment for materialistic things.

Perplexing colleagues, I returned to the office within a week despite initially taking three weeks' vacation for the wedding. Both our companies graciously offered job opportunities for our spouses, and we opted for my husband's company. The subsequent year involved transitioning jobs, changing visas from tourist to business and H1, renting a single room for accommodation, sleeping on a mat, living alone in Bangalore and celebrating festivals solo. I commuted to the office every day, seven days a week. A notable event during this time was the distressing kidnapping of Dr Rajkumar, during which I had to stay at home without food and water for the entire day.

A year flew by, and I found myself in the US with PP. Our time in the US was a blend of delightful personal experiences and fulfilling professional endeavors. Being at the client's location provided an excellent opportunity to gain insight into the business. Both of us shared a passion for movies and often indulged in unlimited watch deals from Blockbuster and Netflix. Our favorite late-night ritual involved heading out at midnight to return CDs at Blockbuster and relishing cheesy fries at Jack in the Box. The arrival of Netflix CDs by postal mail along with return envelopes, added a unique touch to our entertainment routine. We frequently organized movie nights for friends on weekends, with Las Vegas emerging as our preferred destination for leisure.

Pregnancy was an incredible time for me, brimming with gratitude and energy. I remained dedicated to my work until the very last day and welcomed my baby into the world before my maternity leave officially commenced on a Monday morning. Since no family could come from India, we relied on the support of some wonderful friends. Managing a baby without the usual family and maid support in a foreign country was a bit tough. After a four-month maternity break, I returned to work, and my mom came to help with the family. Recognizing the baby's frailty, she started giving the baby massages, and soon, our little one grew strong and happy.

We relocated from Phoenix to Salt Lake City for work. My mom had to return to India to take care of my ailing grandmother. Our baby started attending daycare. On some lunch breaks, I visited to check on her, and often, the staff informed me she was sleeping, so I returned to work. One day, when I went to check, I found her sobbing under her favorite blanket, the one we fondly called the magic blanket. It is heartbreaking for any parent to witness their baby cry. However, during the evening pickup, she was happily playing. I have immense respect for all the caretakers who looked after my kids, and I will always be grateful to them. After another six months, we decided to go back to India. Everyone in our extended family joined us for our daughter's 1st birthday party at both her grandparents' home. Upon returning to Bangalore, we purchased our first house.

Providing feedback and detailing our preferences to the architect while designing our new house was a special and satisfying experience. Being our first home, we took meticulous care to ensure it was tailored to our comfort. The process of settling into the new house and forming connections within the community became one of the most memorable experiences of our lives.

We were eagerly anticipating the arrival of our second baby, and at the same time, we booked a spacious villa, fulfilling my dream of a dream house. Despite some on-site opportunities, I made it clear that I wouldn't be leaving India. I took a one-year extended leave to look after both babies, while my husband enrolled in the Executive MBA program at IIM Bangalore.

PP went to the UK for an assignment when the second baby was one and a half years old. I had to wait in Bangalore to get the visa for the family and our live-in domestic help Laila. I also had to look for a suitable work opportunity for me in the UK. My domestic help's visa was rejected twice. For the third time, I went to the Chennai consulate with both the babies and the maid, requesting them to relook at the documents, as the reason for rejection provided was not valid. The visa was granted immediately. Sometimes, the help provided by faceless people changes the course of life for someone. I only spoke to a lady on the phone and didn't even go inside the consulate building. I could work full-time in the UK, and Laila could help her family build a house from her UK salary. I went to Marina Beach the second-time to celebrate and then came back to Bangalore, packed our bags, locked our home, and went to the UK.

The flight experience wasn't pleasant. Since my son was under two, he didn't have a seat and couldn't stay on my lap for the entire journey, which some passengers objected to. One lady fellow passenger advised me that I should not give kids chocolate during the journey. I later realized that one aunt who came to see us off bought chocolates, and both my kids had a lot of them on the flight, making them super active when everyone was trying to nap.

Work went well, and life settled in the UK. My kids joined schools, and it surprised me that you need to wait for two months for school admission confirmation. There were no school buses; we had to go by public bus and walk, taking 45 minutes one way to drop my daughter off at school. To open a bank account, even a salary account, I had to stand in a queue for a couple of hours. When they announced lunchtime, I came back without opening the account and called ICICI Bank. They came to our home in the UK and opened our account.

My son, who started his academic journey in the UK, is now enrolling in an undergraduate course in the UK at the world's number one university for sport-related studies. Meanwhile, my daughter has recently finished her undergraduate studies at Shri Ram College of Commerce (SRCC) Delhi, India's premier college for commerce courses, and has now joined the corporate world through her college placement.

Without the on-site opportunities in the US and UK, my exposure to the world and different cultures would have been confined to movies and web series. I wouldn't have had the chance to visit incredible places like Universal Studios, Disneyland, Las Vegas, and London.

C 7.6 From School Bells to City Tales: Scindia Boarding and Settling in Delhi's Rhythm

Another turning point in my life came on January 3rd 2018. My daughter was preparing for her 10th board exams, and my husband had returned from his work-related trip from Gwalior, Madhya Pradesh. He asked our daughter – "Do you want to join India's number one boarding school? It is situated in a lush green space in a heritage building. You will have students from different places. You will not only have academics and sports but drama and social service, too, as part of your curriculum. You will develop confidence and discipline, and you will make friends for life. The school will blossom your personality. You will have a stronger sense of hard work, responsibility, teamwork, and adaptability. Above all, you will have lots of fun." My daughter, who was already looking to change from ICSE to CBSE school in grade 11, embraced the concept of a boarding school wholeheartedly and responded with an enthusiastic "yes".

I tried to convince her that nowadays boarding schools are for kids from smaller towns where there are not many good schools, but in Bengaluru, you are already at the best school that provides all-round development. At home, you enjoy the luxury of a separate room, whereas at the boarding school, you would be residing in a dormitory." She said assertively, "I have already visited almost all the top schools of Bengaluru to play tournaments as part of the school's basketball team", and she said with great pride that none surpasses the excellence of her current school." I found myself mentally unprepared to send my daughter anywhere, let alone to Gwalior, a considerable 3000 kilometers away from Bengaluru.

The following week, my husband called from Delhi, mentioning that he was getting his grandmother's small house painted, which we were utilizing as our company's guest house. He informed me that he would be traveling to Delhi frequently this year. With Lohri, a favorite festival among Punjabis, around the corner, and our recent shift to a 7-star villa property in Bengaluru near our kids' school, I wished to introduce our neighborhood, predominantly consisting of Keralaites, to the joy of our Punjabi festivities. Realizing there wasn't sufficient time to gather funds, I inquired with one of the Resident Welfare Association (RWA) members about the budget availability for organizing the Lohri party. She conveyed that the RWA had no funds and suggested gathering contributions from North Indian residents. This revelation was surprising to me; after spending half my life in Bengaluru, I considered myself more of a Bengalurian than a North Indian. I organized the festival with great energy, and the majority of the residents in our 80+ villa community enthusiastically participated, making the event a resounding success.

The residential complex boasted nearly every state-of-the-art facility imaginable: expansive basketball, football, squash, and badminton courts, a well-equipped gym, an outdoor and indoor heated pools, a furnished party hall, an amphitheater, guest rooms, lush green gardens, a dog park, fountains, and more. My son's preferred spots were the football ground and the pool, where he spent most of his day playing. One day, as I watched his game, I called my husband in Delhi and posed the question – can we all move to Delhi? To my surprise, he agreed. Having moved to Bangalore at 22, we had never contemplated leaving this city. We then consulted our 12-year-old son, asking if he wanted to study in India's top boarding school, located in a 6th-century fort. The boy's school was separate from the girls' school, meaning he wouldn't be able to meet his sister regularly. Despite this, he enthusiastically said yes.

On April 20th, we embarked on our road journey from Bengaluru to Delhi in our Scorpio, visiting friends and family along the way and reaching Delhi on May 1st, 2018. The kids joined Scindia boarding school at the end of June. This marked a major change in their lives – from separate bedrooms to dorms, pleasant year-round weather to extreme climates, a comfortable lifestyle to 5 a.m. wake-ups and runs, and an English-speaking environment to Hindi-speaking surroundings and transitioning from a flexible family environment to strict discipline. Despite these changes, both kids cherished their boarding school experiences and recommend everyone consider joining a boarding school. The message is clear, we should not resist change; it brings with it vibrant experiences.

Had we not relocated to Delhi, we would have missed out on the opportunity to reside in the capital of India, the very heart of the nation. Exploring the culture and various attractions of Delhi turned out to be a delightful experience. The holistic experience of boarding school helped children develop adaptability and interpersonal and leadership skills.

Chapter 8

Family First Always

"I sustain myself with the love of my family"

**– Maya Angelou, Renowned poet,
author and civil rights activist**

"Family is a life jacket in the stormy sea of life"

**– J. K. Rowling, British author,
best known for the Harry Potter series**

The entrepreneurial journey is demanding and involves long working hours and high levels of stress. The support and understanding from family members act as a source of inspiration and a driving force for founders. A strong family foundation provides emotional stability and motivation. Prioritizing family ensures a support system during challenging times, helps maintain a work-life balance and promotes personal well-being, which is crucial for sustained creativity, productivity, and overall success in the challenging world of startups. The desire to create a better future for one's family can serve as a powerful motivator, encouraging founders to overcome obstacles and achieve success.

C 8.1 Strong Family Support

We need strong family support. Our family members provide unconditional love and you can always rely on them. You can discuss any problem and find a solution together.

We must listen patiently to family members and understand what they are going through without judging them. We should always be ready to help them. My family was my biggest support. They were always ready to help. They helped us financially and emotionally. They were always there to pray for me and support me. When you know that there is someone who has your best interest in mind, you feel blessed. All the problems look small. It gives you the courage and confidence to face all the challenges that life throws at you.

In India, large families bonding over food and having fun at functions, festivals and family get-togethers are a very common sight and we are proud of our culture. In some families, they discuss politics and people, but they don't discuss their problems; they discuss films and food but not their financial issues; they discuss holiday destinations but not their health issues; they discuss weather but do not discuss ways to create wealth, they will have tea together, but there is no mutual trust and transparency, they seldom discuss or feel secure enough to discuss their mental, emotional and financial issues.

When we hesitate to open up and tell our worries to our family members, they do not get any clue about what we are going through. We can always talk to them, make connections, and take them in confidence. It helps us find new perspectives and solutions for our problems. It helps us choose the right path, take corrective action, seek external help, or merely have their support etc. Family members genuinely care about our well-being and feel joy when we make progress. Without family support, and someone to talk to or share our issues with, enduring constant struggles and stress may result in physical and mental ailments.

During her summer vacation in seventh grade, my daughter expressed the desire to contribute, so I introduced her to online banking. She took on responsibilities like managing salary transfers, vendor payments, submitting provident fund forms, and depositing the amount for each employee through the government portal. Each day, she diligently cleared pending payments from the accountant's spreadsheet and marked them as paid. She also observed the challenges we faced, such as despite clear instructions to pay invoices promptly, for large payments we had to wait for days due to the non-availability of funds and delay in receiving payments from our clients.

On a grocery shopping trip to Total Mall, my younger one headed toward KFC with the shopping cart. Quick to remind him of our financial commitments, my daughter held his hand, guided him away, and explained, "We cannot have food here; it's already the 28th, and Daddy and Mumma have to pay salaries on the 1st."

While impressed by her thoughtfulness, I couldn't shake off the mother's guilt of exposing her to our financial challenges so early in life. I began to question my decision to involve her in the business and took back the responsibility of handling all financial transactions myself. On her subsequent vacation, she contributed by recording her voice for a tourism app we developed for the Rajasthan government. The family inevitably gets involved in the business; it gives them the confidence and satisfaction of being of some help, and despite efforts to keep them away, challenges impact everyone in some way or another.

C 8.2 Friends are Overrated, Networking is Non-Reliable

While there are countless examples of strong friendships, I can't help but think that friends are often overrated. They seem to be around solely for the good times and tend to shy away when you're facing challenges. Some believe that personal issues should be left within the family sphere.

We spend a considerable amount of time with friends engaging in various enjoyable activities like partying, dancing, and having fun. We like gossiping with them, going out with them, and playing games with them. Yes, they help us to have great times but their support through bad times is often lacking. It seems they consider such matters as family concerns, leaving families to shoulder the responsibility. They will come up with excuses when asked for help.

Throughout our lives, we form many friendships in college, organizations, neighborhoods, and through social media. However, it might be more worthwhile to prioritize family time and personal growth over excessive socializing. Taking responsibility for ourselves and minimizing expectations from others is a valuable lesson.

Some founders distance themselves from friends due to the fear of being judged. They prefer to cope with challenges by isolating themselves. If your founder friends have not been communicating with anyone for a long time, consider reaching out to them.

Networking events are organized to reach out to fellow members and collaborate with the community. In my experience, networking events often revolve around self-promotion and offer limited opportunities for collaboration and co-creation. While it's always enjoyable to listen to great speakers, meet event organizers, exchange ideas, participate in panel discussions, and gain new insights, the collaborative aspect is frequently overlooked. It's crucial for individuals to actively seek out opportunities to contribute their skills, expertise, and perspectives, ensuring a two-way exchange that benefits both personal growth and creates a more enriching networking experience for all participants.

C 8.3   Parenting is the Greatest Joy

Parenting is the greatest joy. Parenting is pure love and devotion, you give to your kids and receive from them. It cannot be compared to anything. I consider myself fortunate to have two beautiful souls as my children, and I feel blessed each day.

The bond between a mother and her kids is incredibly strong. A mother feels responsible for raising her kids who become kind and caring adults. Prioritizing the well-being of the family is a woman's foremost commitment. There is immense satisfaction in taking care of the family, planning for kids' education, cooking for them, making every day special, and taking an active part in their growing up years. My bedtime ritual includes reflecting on golden moments spent with my family during the day. These moments create lasting memories and add cherished chapters to my life book.

Working full-time and taking care of the family with the support of maids were the best years of my life. I am grateful to my domestic helps, who were with me in that special phase of my life.

Creating a positive home environment filled with love, laughter, and support during stressful times could be challenging and it becomes a significant test for the women of the house. I found that promoting self-care for each family member, incorporating elements like love, patience, meditation, yoga, breathing exercises, reading, and journaling, was immensely beneficial in successfully handling those challenging days.

Even if someone doesn't have their biological kids, adopting children or getting involved in social causes can bring the same amount of happiness and satisfaction.

C 8.4 Live a Luxurious Life with Limited Resources

Even with limited finances, one can lead a fulfilling life by doing enriching activities such as reading, writing, and participating in events. Fortunately, being in Delhi provided me with ample opportunities and access to events organized by the Central government and private organizations.

Effective time management is essential. Learning from individuals who have been in similar situations and drawing inspiration from admired leaders by watching their speeches and attending live events can be highly beneficial. Exploring public parks, historical sites, museums, and temples is not only enjoyable and refreshing but also budget-friendly. These visits serve as excellent distractions from life's challenges, offering opportunities for learning, networking and finding solutions to your problems.

The government regularly hosts exhibitions, while cultural evenings at public venues and business events organized by media companies and corporates are also prevalent. I began attending some of these events and enrolled in various courses, some of which were free or charged nominal fees. This approach allowed me to fully enjoy life without feeling financially constrained.

Information about events and exhibitions can be found on social media and in newspapers, so keep an eye out for such opportunities. Various cultural evenings are organized by embassies, government offices, ministries of tourism and culture, etc.

By not taking advantage of available resources, one may feel like a victim, which may lead to emotional disturbances and difficulty in clearing mental hurdles if they arise.

C 8.5 Enhancing Employee Experience: From Bring Your Kids to Work to Festive Galas

Big organizations implement various initiatives to enhance employee satisfaction. One of the initiatives is to bring your kids to work day. They celebrate all festivals of all religions and regions with great enthusiasm. There are many celebrations on the organization's special days, such as Founder's Day, key visits by global heads and leaders, achievement of significant milestones, etc. These help employees and their families feel connected and valued by the organization.

These festivals feature a lot of fun games, quizzes, food stalls, marketplaces, promotional events, talks, competitions, etc. Employees often dress in their traditional outfits. One can see the cultural diversity in these events. They provide a great platform for individuals with artistic minds to express themselves through artwork, rangolis, and collages, and demonstrate skills in photography, music, dance, event management, event hosting etc. These festivities are great opportunities for networking, stress-busting, work-life balancing, displaying extraordinary skills and reigniting extra-curricular hobbies.

These initiatives are approved by top leadership, spearheaded by the human resources department, supported by organizational leaders, carried out by volunteers across various departments, and are thoroughly enjoyed by all the employees and their families. Such events help create strong bonds among employers, employees, and their families.

Without these activities, employees' families miss out on the firsthand opportunity to understand and appreciate the work, culture, team dynamics, and office environment. This weakens the bond between the organization and its employees, leading to increased dissatisfaction.

C 8.6 Family that Cooks Together and Eats Together, Stays Together

In every culture, families unite through the love of food. "Families that cook together and eat together stay together."

This timeless wisdom highlights the bond created through preparing and enjoying meals together. Food gives us energy and happiness. This daily tradition helps create a strong bond with our family and provides a sense of belonging and security to each family member.

Incorporate a diverse range of foods, including the favorite dishes of your family members, into your daily menus. Try out new recipes, and explore new restaurants and local cuisines for more fun. Baking and BBQ parties at home are great ways to connect with family and friends. Celebrate birthdays, festivals, and achievements to share quality time, reinforce communication, and strengthen and build family bonds. Studies have shown that eating meals together has a positive effect on children's physical and mental well-being. They learn important social skills and have higher self-esteem. If you have any medical conditions, eat food as prescribed.

Prioritizing and valuing family mealtime in our daily schedule is crucial. Enjoy the cooking time as if cooking were a meditation. Occasionally, do elaborate meal preparation. Appreciate the efforts put in by family members to cook. We must appreciate simple food, too. Gratitude and respect toward food should never be forgotten. Also, keep moderation in mind so that we do not overindulge in food, harm our health, impact our productivity, and slow our self-growth.

It's essential to schedule and prepare our meals at home thoughtfully. Otherwise, the fun will be missing from life, and without proper nutrition, we may experience constant lethargy and laziness.

C 8.7   Got Married into the Famous Bhatnagar Family of India's Great Scientist Sir Shanti Swarup Bhatnagar

It was a proud moment for me when I got married into the family of a famous scientist of India, Sir Shanti Swarup Bhatnagar. An eminent scientist, Sir S S Bhatnagar, is recognized for his contribution to developing post-independent India's science and technology infrastructure and policies. He was an Indian colloid chemist, academic and scientific administrator. The highest scientific award in India is given in his name. He was the founder of the Council of Scientific and Industrial Research (CSIR) organization. He is also revered as the "father of research laboratories" in India. He was also the first Chairman of the University Grants Commission (UGC). He was a respected author and poet, too. His collection of poetry was published in a book named 'Lajwanti', which was dedicated to his wife. He also wrote the Kulgeet of Banaras Hindu University.

My husband is a great-grandson of Sir S S Bhatnagar. The family had a strong history of highly qualified individuals, with members educated in esteemed universities outside India. My Punjabi business-class family was delighted to be associated with such a highly educated family.

We knew each other through a mutual friend and we became pen friends in our college days. It's worth noting that pen friendships, a term unfamiliar to the current generation, were a cherished part of our school days. I fondly recall the thrill of receiving letters and photographs from pen friends in New York and New Zealand.

PP and I got our posting together in Bangalore.

True to his legacy, PP stands out as the most intelligent, knowledgeable, sincere, hardworking, and technically skilled person I have encountered throughout my 27-year career. His profound and diverse understanding spans subjects such as science, technology, finance, foreign policies, politics, books, and movies, consistently leaving me in awe. His expertise extends to the rapid creation of proposals, presentations, pricing models, agreements, Excel, and MPP work, as well as exploring new technologies and gazettes. Whether understating design to delivering products and services, giving presentations to clients, understanding their needs, patiently addressing their queries for weeks, consulting, engaging in sales and marketing, negotiating, or managing relationships with clients, employees, ex-colleagues, and classmates, PP excels in every aspect. His talents also extend beyond the professional realm, evident in his exceptional skills in driving, cooking, hosting guests, singing, and playing musical instruments. He loves reading novels, and articles, and listening to podcasts. His ability to manage stress and bounce back serves as a remarkable example for startup founders. I watched such a deserving individual work tirelessly for 12-14 hours a day for years without complaining even during the most challenging times of our startup journey. Tears welled up in my eyes as I wrote this paragraph.

PP is also a compassionate person. During his long commutes between meetings at client locations in Bengaluru, he would occasionally stop to eat at roadside food vans. This incident took place before demonetization and the Covid era, when digital payments were not as widely accepted as they are today. On one such occasion, a disabled beggar approached him, and he, with only Rs 50 in his wallet, generously gave it to the beggar, choosing to remain hungry.

As part of one of our startups, He also ventured into agriculture, leasing 8 acres of land for seven years to cultivate papayas and bananas. The resulting produce was even exported to neighboring countries. His dedication, commitment, and enthusiasm in working with diverse clients, ranging from the world's largest banks and automotive clients to Chinese and Taiwanese vendors, chip makers, local component vendors, and senior bureaucrats in the government, as well as farmers, continue to impress me to this day.

PP is deeply passionate about social causes. Through, one of our startups, he provided funding and support to the not-for-profit NGO, Navachetana, which operated microfinance programs in Haveri, Karnataka. Navachetana aimed to uplift marginalized and BPL households by offering micro-loans to women, empowering them to establish small businesses. However, the NGO's original business model faced sustainability challenges; with minimal inputs from donations and grants, they could not expand. PP played a pivotal role in transforming its mindset from a non-profit to a for-profit set-up and implemented robust processes for operations, IT, risk management, HR, and statutory reporting. With assistance, the NGO's revenue surged from 40 lakhs to 20 crores within a few years, becoming a for-profit enterprise that could positively impact the lives of thousands of women. While retaining the pristine organizational values of social empowerment, the organization also became more professional, adept at fundraising, and automated in its loan and collection processes.

There were some ups and downs during the struggling days. Financial challenges bring with them various family issues. Amidst it all, I held onto the belief that I am precisely where I need to be and that the best is yet to come.

Chapter 9

Tools and Techniques to Triumph Through Tough and Trying Times

"We must accept finite disappointment, but we must never lose infinite hope."

– Martin Luther King, Jr, American civil rights leader and inspirational speaker

Incorporating both spiritual and physical practices benefits founders by reducing stress and helping them stay focused. The simple tools and techniques help founders stay centered and emotionally balanced as they go through challenges in their startup journey. Practices like gratitude journaling encourage a positive mindset, helping founders find silver linings even in adversity. Mindfulness meditation helps reduce stress and enhances focus, allowing founders to make clearer decisions. Having clarity about yourself and what is happening internally with your thoughts, beliefs, feelings, and decisions is what separates amazing leaders from good leaders. Engaging in regular exercise not only contributes to physical well-being but also releases endorphins, boosting mood and resilience. Together, these tools and techniques contribute to the overall health and mental strength of founders and their families as they meet the ever-growing demands of running a startup.

C 9.1   Unlocking Daily Magic: Setting Intentions, Journaling and Mind Dumps

Setting your daily intentions can be a powerful practice for shaping your day. Maintaining an attitude of gratitude raises your frequency and purifies your aura. Journaling and mind dumping provide the mental clarity essential for a successful day.

As part of my morning routine, I ask myself: 1) What do I want to receive today? 2) What do I want to give today? 3) How do I want to feel today? 4) What do I want to become today? 5) What do I want to achieve today? 6) How do I want to make others feel today? Answering these journaling prompts helped me take better control of my day and my life.

While you set your intentions for the day, support your thoughts and desires with pure intent, then believe and surrender to the almighty. With consistent practice, you will witness the transformation of your life. Pure intent is required to manifest what you visualize and what you dream of. Intent to love, care, heal, help, and willingness to give back will help you strengthen relationships. Once you take charge of your relations and emotions consciously, work, and everything else will go well.

These ideas also support the law of equilibrium, where you want to give and receive both. I learned this and a few other techniques from Luke Coutinho. I started writing Morning Pages, the three pages as suggested by Julia Cameron in her book "The Artist's Way."I started following the golden hour of a 20-minute walk-in the park, 20 minutes of reading, and 20 minutes of pranayama and meditation. I started capturing the golden moments of the day; they would add pages to my memory book. I learned these and many other golden techniques from Dr. Shivangi Maletia. I started appreciating small wins and nurturing my spiritual growth.

These are the magical activities sure to bring magic into your life. The absence of these in your life will create more worries and suffering.

C 9.2 Sunshine, Spending Time in Nature and Talking to Trees

To feel refreshed, alert, and energized when we wake up in the morning, we must go out in the sunshine. We can spend some time in nature if possible. Get the sunlight through a window if going out is not possible. This will help us get our circadian rhythm and center ourselves. Even if we go out and do nothing in the sunshine, that is fine.

Circadian rhythm is the 24-hour cycle by which all your cells operate, and the coordinated timing of these operations is guided primarily by light. As soon as we wake up, we must soak in some sunshine, even if it's only for 5 minutes. Please do not touch your phone even to access your workout and meditation apps. You will see some amazing benefits – balanced eating, sleep, social life, work-life balance, hormones, better mental and physical health, relationships, brain function, bone health, digestion, blood circulation, and immunity. When our eyes are exposed to a lot of sunlight during the day, the body responds by producing even more melatonin at night, ensuring deep and restorative sleep.

We can make nature our best friend. Tell your problems to your favorite tree If you do not have anyone to share your problems with. Next time near your house, find your favorite tree to talk to about all your problems and give all your worries to Mother Earth. When you go for a walk, try to observe new things, even if it's on the same path. Notice the new flower that has come into bloom. Any more fruits on the guava tree on your walk to the park? Observers, and it will help you be mindful. Your worries will run away, and your mood will be instantly uplifted.

Engage in gardening to stay connected with nature. Caring for plants not only helps the environment but also provides a therapeutic and rewarding experience to you, and you enjoy the beauty, calmness, and contentment that comes from nurturing life through gardening.

Staying away from nature and sunshine can result in accumulated stress, overthinking, and serious health issues.

C 9.3   Deep Breathing, Box Breathing, and Pranayam

A little conscious breathwork daily is very important for your body. It clears toxins from the body and helps you stay calm in stressful situations. Deep breathing, box breathing and pranayams are powerful techniques to remove anxiety and provide holistic health.

Try doing belly breathing, also called diaphragmatic breathing. Place your hand on the abdomen and inhale deeply by expanding your belly like a balloon, and then hold your breath for 6-12 seconds and exhale deeply by contracting your belly to your spine. You can choose to do belly breathing any time before your meals, after your meals, when you wake up, and before you sleep.

Belly breathing has numerous other benefits. It will help in weight management by reducing your cravings, will help in stress management by bringing down your cortisol levels, will improve the quality of your sleep, keep our immunity strong by ensuring oxygen reaches every cell of the body, will strengthen the digestive system, will help reverse aging by increasing the production of human growth hormone and will improve our mental focus by moving us to alpha and theta wavelengths where we are calmer.

Box breathing is a breathing technique you can practice to make you feel energized instantly. It is called square breathing, where you inhale-hold-exhale-hold for a count of 4 or 5. In six repetitions, you will feel the energy. It will slow down your breathing. It works by distracting your mind as you count to four, calming your nervous system, and decreasing stress in your body. It also helps clear your mind and return your focus and concentration. You can-do this anytime, anywhere. It's beneficial when done before your meeting, talk, etc.

Pranayama such as *Kapalbhati, Anulom Vilom, Bhastrika and Bhramri* are great for your overall health. They bring harmony among the body, mind, and spirit, making one physically, mentally and spiritually strong. Practicing pranayams makes one energetic, enthusiastic, calmer and more positive. Such a state of mind helps us make better decisions, provides mental strength while dealing with adversities, and makes us feel happier. It brings clarity to the mind and good health to the body.

These simple exercises will provide tremendous benefits. Some of these techniques can be done in the office, too, if we do not practice these simple exercises. It will impact our performance, lung capacity and cognitive ability.

C 9.4 Harnessing Nature's Power: Watching Sunrise for Energy and Moongazing for Calmness

Watching the sunrise and gazing at the moon are very powerful activities. The sun provides you with instant energy, and moon gazing will fill you with calm. They inspire us to be like them. The sun is always helping something or someone grow. It is always sharing and helping others grow. The light of the moon keeps us safe in the darkness. It reminds us that there is always a light waiting for us to hold onto, even when everything seems dark, even when it seems like the end is coming.

The first ray of the sun gives you hope that no matter what, after darkness, there is always light. The sun will shine and give his blessings. Greet the sun and express gratitude for a new day in your life. Say all your affirmations, spread your arms like SRK's signature dance step, and declare to the world that you are a good mother, good human being, good employer, good team member, good author, or whatever you want to be. The moon reflects beauty even with all its imperfections. It gives you a reason to shine and smile even in the darkness, even when you are alone. Take inspiration and have belief in yourself and God. Always keep faith that success is not far from you.

Just like the moon controls the tides, it impacts us, too, as our bodies are also made up of 70% water. The full moon gives extra light to the sky and extra energy to us. It may arouse violent emotions and behavior in some people. Do meditation to keep a relaxed and open mind. Find your best mindset and focus on pushing out the negative. Full moon meditations are also a great time to connect to your inner world and set intentions. It will help you think clearly, will sharpen your intellect, and calm your nervous system.

If we do not take time to observe the sun or the moon, God's natural blessings for mankind, our growth in emotional, mental, and spiritual areas will be negatively impacted.

C 9.5   A Holistic Approach to Well-Being: Mindfulness, Meditation, Flow State and Sound Sleep

Mindfulness, meditation, flow state, and good sleep are important pillars for holistic health. They help you balance emotions and manage anger. They provide you with mental clarity to achieve your goals and dreams and to take certain actions that can reduce your stress and anxiety over time.

Wherever possible, practice mindfulness in your daily routine. Strive to do routine activities with mindfulness. Spend some quiet time daily with yourself. Flow is our natural state, but we resist it; sometimes, our ego resists the flow state to protect us. Stay in the state of flow, and you will glow from within. Sleep is the best medicine for you. Always talk positively to yourself. Accept whatever you cannot control, or let go if you cannot accept.

Positive self-talk, meditation, practicing gratitude, accepting and appreciating people around us, spending time with loved ones, laughing, resting, spending time in nature, and living with consciousness, awareness, and mindfulness allow us to be in a state of flow. With awareness, we can take the right action. Go out in nature, where there are no distractions. Your anxiety and stress will get better. You will have mental clarity to achieve your goals, which is an important leadership skill. You can finish a task efficiently, faster, and with a sense of fulfillment. All forms of meditation will help calm your nervous system, reduce stress and anxiety, make better decisions, feel happier, save a lot of energy and deal with life's many challenges. With mindfulness, learn to feel and connect with your breath, body, thoughts, and emotions, and you will be able to connect with people better, and your focus will improve. You will also be able to respond to life's complex situations with calm and clarity.

The energy you sleep with is the energy you wake up with. The emotions and thoughts you carry into sleep will directly affect the mood and mindset you will have the next day. Clean up your mind before going to bed. Clear unresolved issues and thoughts in your head by writing them down. Favor your health by forgiving people from your heart. Let go of worries and go to sleep as if feeling relaxed and cleansed. You can also meditate before going to bed. Sit quietly, observe your thoughts without judging or labeling them and create space in your mind. Resolve anything that is bothering you and release all grudges or other negative states. Read a book, practice gratitude, or think about activities and events you're looking forward to. End your day with something that makes you feel good, like a small win or accomplishment. Keep it simple. A win could be anything from reading one page of a book to making a successful presentation to a client. Do this every night and notice positive changes in your life.

I'm grateful to the mentors and social media influencers I follow for their amazing teachings. Without these activities, You may continue to lead a stressful life. You may have a disharmony in your relationships. Diseases will be with you without you even noticing them or inviting them.

C 9.6   Path to Success: Self-Belief, Faith, Gratitude, and Humble Attitude

All the power you need resides within you. Always trust your abilities. The attitude of gratitude keeps us grounded. Humility helps us keep our egos in control.

You're a unique person. Believe in yourself. Trust that you can-do anything. What is possible for others is possible for you, too. God has planned good things for you. You may have self-doubt, and you may have a lot of questions, but always choose faith over fear. Always pray with faith and belief and surrender. Become one with the universe.

Reprogram your subconscious mind with positive affirmations. Identify your highest value, which is the most meaningful and serves as your purpose, being most present and consistent in your life. You don't need motivation for this; it comes from within. It gives you the most fulfillment. Hold the belief you are worth more and that you deserve it. The key is to realize that it's all possible and not as far away as you think. Understand your priorities, focusing on what you genuinely want. Connect with yourself and acknowledge that achieving your goals is within reach.

Practice meditation to reduce cortisol levels, alleviate pain, boost your immune system, and enhance your inner peace.

Meditation can induce and sustain alpha brain waves, indicative of high-level emotional, mental, and spiritual integration. Carrying elevated mental states into waking consciousness, visualize a bright future, immerse yourself in the associated emotions, and remain in that positive state. Embracing smiles and laughter acts as powerful medicines. Cultivate humility to develop close connections and empower those around you. Express gratitude for what you have, and exhibit kindness and compassion toward others.

If you lack self-belief, embarking on a startup journey may be challenging. Along the way, you will encounter many individuals who will doubt, question, mock, obstruct, misguide, demotivate and mistreat you and tell you that you are a failure. Let the haters fuel you; the best founders have failed and found the courage to push through. Only with self-belief, you will be able to hang on for a longer time. Even when every other factor is working against you, your ability to persevere alone will determine your success. Develop the ability to deal with success and failure with equanimity. Always stay humble, aim high, and fly high. This approach will simplify life and free you from unnecessary worries and anxiety.

C 9.7 Your Fitness Choices: 7k Steps, Yoga and Zumba

Start with simplicity. Dedicate 30 minutes to exercise each day. Whether it's taking 7000 steps, practicing Zumba, or indulging in yoga, choose an activity that resonates with you. This routine will infuse you with increased energy, vitality, and confidence.

Some of the best practices I learned are 10 minutes of walking after 20 minutes of every meal and 45 minutes of the Common Yoga Protocol (CYP) routine. CYP, developed by the Ministry of Aayush, comprises day-to-day yoga practice to reap the benefits of yoga. The protocol intends to create a general awareness of how to attain peace, harmony, and well-being through yoga practices such as Asanas, Yoga Nidra, Pranayama, Dhyana, etc. If you are seeking a lively and enjoyable workout, explore Zumba or dance-based workouts. The fusion of upbeat music and workouts instantly elevates your mood and energizes you. For those inclined toward outdoor activities, consider joining a gym, playing a sport, or participating in sports-related events such as marathons or 5k Runs.

These activities can be done anywhere. Join physical or online classes, and you will become more regular with your practice. You can also practice on your own by watching videos. The consistency will yield considerable results. Your mind and soul will be balanced, and your concentration and quality of thought will improve. Your emotions will be balanced, too, and your body weight will be in control. Relationships will improve, and you will become a more efficient, empathetic, inspiring, and productive leader. You will witness the benefits in every area of your life. Place a high value on your health, making it a top priority, and this will inspire steadfast dedication to your exercise routine.

Failure to engage in physical exercise can lead to an imbalance in your body, mind, and soul, potentially contributing to the development of diseases.

Chapter 10

Activities to Ace Bad Days

"Many of life's failures are people who did not realize how close they were to success when they gave up."

– Thomas Edison, Light bulb inventor

Engaging in activities to overcome challenging days is vital for founders and their families as it safeguards mental well-being and promotes sustainable performance. These activities enable founders to manage setbacks effectively, maintain a focused and healthy mindset, and prevent burnout. Seeking support and incorporating stress-relief strategies contribute to enhanced problem-solving skills, promoting innovation and creativity. Ultimately, these activities are essential for founders to lead with resilience, make informed decisions, and sustain long-term success in the dynamic and demanding landscape of entrepreneurship.

C 10.1 Influencer and Motivational Speakers, Life Coaches and Mentor Support

Listening to influencers, motivational speakers, life coaches, and mentors is a wonderful way to keep learning and growing. They inspire you to act and progress fast. They help you see the world from a different perspective.

Excellent support is available through mentors. Enroll in their paid courses and join them in their live sessions. Interact with community members and complete assignments and challenges. Learn new skills. Stay away from the issues that are bothering you and are beyond your control, and channel your efforts into constructive activities. The energy in group classes is infectious. It helps you to create and share your knowledge. Join the VIP community of some of the leading mentors and learn from them; the learning curve will be faster. Learn from people who are a few steps ahead of you. They provide you with guidance that may help in your personal and business growth. Add value by sharing your experiences and learnings. These are some of the effective ways to keep away stress caused by uncertainty. The confidence you get by completing certificates, cohorts, challenges, etc., helps you confront situations in your life in a better way.

Getting a mentor will save you years of effort and frustration. They can alter the course of your life in a few minutes. Start engaging and sharing your story of struggles, wins, and failures. Choose a mentor, based on your needs, someone who can give you support, direction, and confidence.

Without any support system, the likelihood of falling into depression increases, which can only be cured through professional counseling and medicines. Stress and anxiety are best handled through counseling and by practicing relaxation techniques.

C 10.2 Fun Road Trips

Relaxation, spending quality time with family, and creating new experiences can all be achieved through road trips.

We've been fortunate to explore a wide range of places across India, from hill stations, temple towns and beautiful beaches to coffee and tea estates. We covered a lot of places; one memorable moment was hitting the 100,000-kilometer mark on our Scorpio during our trip to the Halebid temples; the excitement was incredible. We've made lasting memories on our journeys.

One of our most unforgettable and longest trips was the move from Bengaluru to Delhi. It was emotional as we were leaving behind the place we'd called home, the city that was our "karmbhumi" for over two decades. We covered the distance in 10 days with our loyal dog Poppins by our side. Along the way, we visited different towns, friends, and family. India's road infrastructure is impressive, and we're big fans of road trips. PP is a skilled driver, and we feel safest with him at the wheel.

We are privileged to have been born in a great country that is rich in natural beauty and diversity. With mountains, beaches, deserts, monuments, world heritage sites, rivers, walking tracks, and colorful heritage cities, there is so much to explore and enjoy and learn about our rich culture and civilization.

These fun trips add excitement and variety to our lives. Without these adventures, life could become monotonous. Without any outings to look forward to, the work-life balance is difficult to maintain. Without exposure to road trips and trips in general, kids will not be well-prepared to take on the world when they grow up.

C 10.3   Love for Cricket and Cinema

Our deep love for cricket and cinema is rooted in our culture. These two passions have been a part of our upbringing, and watching them together has created strong bonds within our families.

Whether it's Bollywood, Hollywood, world cinema or web series, I have shared the experience of watching them all with my family. Watching old classics and discussing stories related to movies or talking about world history are our favorite activities. Some movies, like the Bond franchise, Mission Impossible, and Back to the Future series, have been watched multiple times. Amitabh Bachchan, with whom I feel a special bond as he is from Allahabad, too, holds a special place in our hearts. We have seen all his movies, especially Agnipath and Sooryavansham, at least 50 times. We still watch Zindagi Na Milegi Dobara every few months. My personal favorites are romantic movies. I fondly remember taking the first half off from work during my kids' holidays to catch the first day, the first show of the new releases. Kids have grown up, and I occasionally visit the cinema hall alone. My daughter rightly said that not all her knowledge comes from textbooks alone; some of her valuable learnings come from watching world cinema.

Two months of IPL's schedule mostly coincided with kids' summer break, and the last-minute excitement in matches kept us glued to the TV. We are still big fans of RCB, and every season, we hope for the team to win the cup. My son, a dedicated footballer, introduced me to late-night football matches, and I became a great fan of Ronaldo. I also admire Nita Ambani for promoting sports and cultural activities in our country.

Sports and cinema play a vital role in providing employment, entertainment, and delightful experiences to everyone. They provide a much-needed distraction and a zing to day-to-day living. People from any spectrum of society can indulge in them and feel rejuvenated. Life would be dull without them.

I did not play any sports while growing up, but our school had a strong basketball team, and I admired its players for their energy, enthusiasm, and attitude. Later, as a parent, I felt immense pride when my daughter represented her school and state in various basketball tournaments. I felt super excited when my son enrolled in a sports management course at the world's no-one university for sports-related programs in the UK. I had the privilege of watching a lot of interschool matches. Watching both my kids play sports gives me great satisfaction.

One day, while walking my dog near the closed-down supermarket in our apartment complex, I had the idea to convert the space into a place for kids' classes. I rented the place, collaborated with teachers from various fields, reached out to Asian Paints for painting services, and furnished it with tables, chairs, mats, almirahs, musical instruments, speakers and boards. Teachers began offering classes in Art, Abacus, Chess, Guitar, Keyboard, Kannada, Hindustani and Carnatic music, Bharatanatyam, and Bollywood dance. Witnessing kids come to the center and learn new skills brought me immense satisfaction. The teachers were equally pleased to have a beautiful place to share their knowledge.

Organizing chess tournaments, where around 100 kids participated, felt like a significant achievement. Collaborating with expert teachers and artists remains one of the most fulfilling experiences of my life.

C 10.4 Explore Events, Exhibitions, Museums and Markets, Plays and Dramas, Nature Walks, Amrit Udhyan

"People often think that something "far off" will make them happy. Moving to a new place, getting a different job, or meeting someone new will change how they feel. But happiness will always be withheld if you believe it is somewhere else. The secret is to find happiness in the people and places that are close to you. See the beauty in the things that are nearby."

– James Clear, Author Atomic Habits

Discovering the gems in your vicinity not only adds a touch of adventure to your routine but also opens doors to hidden treasures. Exploring events, exhibitions, art galleries, museums, markets, theaters, biodiversity parks, and nature trails can provide a welcome escape from work-related stress. These experiences offer the opportunity to witness the beauty of nature, exceptional artistic performances, handcrafted treasures, and cutting-edge technology from India and around the world.

Many events require registration or invitations, ensuring limited crowds for well-organized showcases of the finest global talent. Delhi hosts lots of international events, global trade fairs, world book fairs, musical concerts, literary, spiritual and religious fests, auto shows, etc, with extensive preparations. Delhi also hosts weekly bazaars, book markets, and events organized by foreign embassies and the Ministry of Cultural Affairs for special occasions. You can immerse yourself in a variety of such gatherings, connecting with the broader world both externally and within.

Delhi boasts several captivating places to explore, including the newly renovated Kartvya Path, India Gate, memorials of national leaders, Amrit Udyan at Rashtrapati Bhawan, art galleries, museums, and various parks. You can enjoy Ramlila performances, katas, plays, flower shows, yoga and meditation sessions and experience glimpses of diverse world cultures, forgotten handicraft traditions, enchanting musical performances, and captivating dance shows.

Having something to look forward to is essential to prevent boredom and promote personal growth.

C 10.5 Discover Diverse Spaces: Temples, Parks, Salons, Cafes and State Bhawans

Everyone must explore nearby locations and enhance life. Visiting temples, parks, cafes, salons, commercial complexes, and state bhawan of state governments is a simple way to socialize without social media, connect to the higher power, feel relaxed and boost your brain health.

Experience your city's rich and diverse cultural and recreational spaces. Indian temples are renowned for their awe-inspiring architecture, splendid sculptures, and intricate carvings. They provide a peaceful sanctuary amidst the hustle and bustle. Appreciate deity decorations and divine embellishments and participate in the daily aarti at the temple.

Go to the shopping complexes of your local community. Purchase from local shopkeepers. Savor aromatic brews and engage in delightful conversations with your family and friends at the cozy corners of the café. Indulge in a spa experience at the salon. Savor the delicious flavors of traditional and regional cuisine at various State Bhawans. Go to the green spaces. Do some exercise in the park's open gyms, take a leisurely walk or enjoy a rejuvenating run or energizing jog. Collaborate with community members and take initiatives to build a sustainable society and contribute to environmental conservation.

To discover a wide range of experiences, schedule these activities in your calendar so that you do not miss them. For easy recall, designate specific days for activities, like keeping Tuesdays for temples. Saturdays are for salon or shopping, Wednesdays are for women-only meet-ups, Fridays are for family outings, and Sundays are for getting some sun outdoors. Include as varied experiences as you can. You may not be able to do all these activities, but try to do whatever interests you more. Beware of stray dogs in your local areas as they may hinder exploration of nearby places on foot.

By incorporating these experiences into our routine, we can keep our traditions and culture alive and we can maintain a healthy and active lifestyle. We can also create more understanding among local communities and can contribute positively to various causes.

There will be very little interaction among local communities without these activities. The next generation will not understand the importance of visiting religious places or cultural centers and their impact on our lives.

C 10.6 Soulful Symphony: Playlist of Teenage Favorite Songs, Motivational Songs, Bhajans, Chants and Instrumental Music

Listening to music is a surefire way to uplift your spirits instantly and bring back cherished memories. Music is a ready-made remedy to change your vibration. Research shows music takes 13 minutes to release sadness and nine to make you happy.

Create a playlist of your favorite songs from your teenage years, motivational songs, bhajans, and the latest favorite hits. Listening to them will help you overcome overthinking and shift your mindset to a more positive state. Music nurtures your mind, bhajans soothe your soul, and motivational songs inspire action. Listen mindfully to uplift your spirits, develop mindfulness, and create an anchor for you. Whenever you are feeling low, listen to your old favorite song and move back to the flow state. Music is a great mood enhancer. It has many other benefits, such as reduced muscle tension, decreased negative thoughts, more peace and contentment and better sleep.

Listen to music on your walks, while driving, cooking, doing household chores, etc. Just a few minutes a day is all you need to keep stress away, feel a sense of relief, feel less overwhelmed, more stable, and less likely to be triggered by an issue.

Not listening to music may limit your emotional expression, stress-relief, social connection, and cultural exposure, impacting overall well-being. Your cognitive abilities may diminish. Life without music will be dull. So, let the melodies be a constant companion for a happier, more harmonious life.

Chapter 11

Personal Branding and Transformation

"It is not the strongest or the most intelligent who will survive but those who can best manage change."

**– Charles Darwin, Biologist,
evolution theory pioneer**

Personal branding is a powerful tool for startup founders. It represents the image and values they wish to convey to their clients, employees, and stakeholders. Transforming one's personal brand involves a strategic alignment of individual strengths, values, and aspirations with the startup's mission and vision. For startup founders, personal transformation often involves cultivating leadership skills, adapting to evolving market demands, and embracing a growth mindset. Successful personal branding and transformation not only elevate the founder's reputation but also contribute significantly to the startup's overall success and market positioning.

C 11.1   Meter Man – Create a Personal Brand

Create your powerful personal brand, build a niche product, and showcase the capabilities and values you provide to the world. We started working on smart energy meters as they have a huge requirement in India. We gained expertise in designing different variants of smart meters and setting up the manufacturing plant. I gave PP the new identity of a "Meter Man."

Your unique values, views, thought leadership, skills, strengths, and qualities, along with your stand on social and political issues, contribution, collaboration, and social media currency will create your brand. Create your brand carefully. Generate content related to your industry, work, experience, learnings, opportunities, future direction, impact on the Indian economy, etc., and publish them on your and your organization's social media profile. Create blog posts or write a book to share insights. Participate in industry forums, connect with like-minded individuals, utilize innovation and incubation platforms of various institutes to share knowledge, and provide feedback to the government on various policies related to manufacturing, customs duty on components, ease of business, etc. Go live on social media and share your valuable experience and dos and don'ts for mid-level corporate folks who are planning to start their own ventures. Highlight your accomplishments, case studies, success stories, projects you have worked on, and courses you have completed and establish yourself as an authority in your field.

If you do not create a brand for yourself or your organization, you may find yourself working in isolation, and the world may not be aware of your work. Your skills and experience will not give you an advantage, and your learning may not benefit anyone. When posting on social media, be mindful of your digital footprint. Remember, you are on social media for a constructive purpose, ignore replying to negative comments or be polite and diplomatic in your replies when needed. Always be mindful and responsibly express your views on controversial topics and sensitive issues.

C 11.2   Goal Setting and Tracking

Einstein said that imagination is more important than knowledge. Have a purpose in life, set ambitious goals, dream big, write your goals, create a plan to achieve them, and consistently measure progress to stay on track.

Identify goals in the major areas of your life where you feel lacking. Always create balance among self, family, and career. Your goals should be such that they should give you happiness, freedom, and growth and satisfy your soul. Break down larger goals into smaller actionable steps. Goals will guide you in the right direction. They will motivate you to take the right actions and create an abundant life for you. You must commit yourself to the process and understand that there will be ups and downs and failures. Learn to fail, and learn to learn from failures. Go back to the process, re-evaluate, and make changes as required in the process. There will always be distractions, but focus, prioritization, and commitment to the process and goals will help you get over the distractions. Train your mind to be flexible and be ready to adapt and change according to the circumstances. This will open many doors of possibilities for you.

Goals will help you transform. Goals will help you progress from a good life to a great life. They will provide you with mental clarity and a sense of achievement and fulfillment. In an organization, everyone needs to know about company goals and the roadmap to accomplish them.

Without setting goals, you will not aspire for bigger things; your life may appear purposeless and directionless. You will not know what you want or what your passion is. You will not look forward to chasing your dreams, and you may slowly slip into anxiety, uncertainty, and depression.

C 11.3   Building Strong Communication and Management Skills

Public speaking and effective communication are powerful tools for leaders. They help you get delighted customers and satisfied stakeholders. Effective communication gives confidence to customers and leaves a great impression on investors, employees, and other stakeholders. Firefighting, issue management, etc., are key tasks of leaders that can be managed with ease. Clear, crisp, concise, and regular communication is important to manage business.

To excel as a leader, you must learn the art of communication, negotiation, active listening, conflict resolution, planning, decision-making, delegation, empowerment, change management, time management, etc.. Invest in courses, learn and implement these skills. You will come across as an honest, transparent, and trustworthy leader. You will be more open to taking feedback, understanding others' perspectives, and making better deals. You will be appreciated for the effort you put into developing these skills.

Confidence is success remembered. You need genuine public speaking experiences in your repertoire that you can readily recall. This extends beyond recent rehearsals for your presentation to any recent impromptu speaking opportunity. Join speaking forums, join X spaces, and say yes to spontaneous speaking opportunities. Get used to being on camera if your presentation is virtual. Speaking opportunities are everywhere; deliver your best each time. Keep your preparation simple, and your delivery will be simple and easier for your audience to comprehend. Put yourself in your audience's shoes; great speakers make it about the audience, always ready to give and share.

There will be misunderstandings, escalations, and a slowdown in growth if we fail to work on soft skills. You will appear more nervous, more defensive, and less likely to accomplish your goals.

C 11.4 Power of Visualization and Affirmation

Our mind and body are one. They are connected and continuously communicate with each other. When we say positive affirmations with conviction, feelings, pure intention, and belief daily and repeatedly, we reprogram our subconscious mind to think positively. That results in a positive effect on our body as well.

Affirmations and visualization provide you with superpowers to make your life abundant. Our subconscious mind does not differentiate between reality and imagination. Create a mental image in your mind that your body is healthy and all your relationships are stronger. This can be applied to every area of your life, workspace, career, business, and relationships. There is no harm in thinking positively. There is no money to be spent on thinking of a positive outcome. Practice these with your mind and heart to transform your life mentally, physically, spiritually, and financially.

Seeing is believing. See success in your mind first, deeply feel it, and wholeheartedly believe it. Believing that anything is possible allows inspiration, enthusiasm, and creativity to flow even when things are uncertain or difficult times arise. Use these simple techniques to create a lifestyle full of prosperity, passion, and purpose. In your morning routine, after your meditation, use 5 – 10 minutes for these two techniques: affirmation and visualization; come back to live-in the present and work purposefully toward achieving your dream life.

Difficult times discourage and demotivate us and create undue fears and worries in our minds. We may end up giving up on our dreams if we don't practice these two awesome practices. Use these simple techniques to create a lifestyle full of prosperity, passion, and purpose.

C 11.5   Mastering Storytelling and Writing for Leaders

There is a lot of emphasis on storytelling and writing skills. As a leader, you must cultivate these two important skills. Delivering the key messages in an engaging way to connect with your audience is an art. Stories serve as a memorable tool for conveying important points and instilling values. It is easier to explain your vision, mission, journey, goals, and policies through stories. Stories will motivate your team to take action.

Leaders are readers, and leaders are storytellers. Maintain a storybank from your experiences, client interactions, successes, failures, travel, etc. We can gather stories by reading books – fiction and non-fiction, newspapers, articles, and journals. Listening to podcasts and interviews and watching TV programs contributes to our narrative collection and offers diverse perspectives. Observing daily situations around us, reflecting on our daily experiences, meeting people, and exploring new places further enrich our storybank, and we can communicate effectively through storytelling in different contexts or situations.

If you use these stories in your interaction with clients, vendors, and employees, you will connect with them better. Develop reading and writing skills. Write a blog or a thread on X to share your knowledge. Write a journal for gratitude, goals, self-compassion, problem-solving, mind mapping, mind dumping, etc., to reflect and get mental clarity. You can also write a book to share wisdom on any topic and to provide deep knowledge.

Practice and perform storytelling whenever you get the opportunity. You will become a great storyteller and a great leader. Your business, technical, and storytelling skills will take your business to greater heights. Without these skills, you may come across as an ineffective leader.

C 11.6   Limit Distraction – Managing OTT Abuse

OTT content often includes the use of offensive language and sometimes promotes physical, verbal, and emotional abuse, especially in the web series that is being made in India. These shows are time-consuming and impact the quality of your work.

Watching OTT web series is addictive because of their gripping plots, effective cliffhangers, eye-catching promotions, star power, discussions on social media, and 24*7 availability. Just for fear of missing out, we end up binge-watching long series and wasting our valuable productive hours and sleep. It fills our minds with undesirable content, makes us lazy and sick due to sleep deprivation, and impacts our behavior. You start using abusive language in your day-to-day life, and it negatively impacts your environment and relationships. The environment plays an important role in our overall well-being. We must limit our OTT consumption, be choosy about what we watch and distance ourselves from negative and depressing news. We must consume the information that is useful for the growth of our businesses, communities, and ourselves. This will uplift our spirits and provide us with renewed energy.

If we limit our consumption of OTT content, we can devote more time to our families, checking on their well-being and understanding their interests, desires, passions, problems, etc. We can work toward our mission and become the person we'd be proud of; we can contribute to a positive change in the world. It's also important to celebrate ourselves, our experiences, successes and victories in the present moment.

Closing Thoughts

In the startup world, challenges, struggles, and success are part of the journey. As you've read through the pages of this book, you've gained insights into the myriad hurdles that entrepreneurs face, from funding challenges to market uncertainties, from building the right team to making profits, from finding a first customer to creating an environment of innovation, from setting up a factory to staying motivated. The list is endless, but keep going and keep believing that every problem has a solution.

The path to success is not a straight line. It's a winding road with twists and turns, and it's in those twists and turns that the most valuable lessons are learned. Struggles can lead to growth. Embrace them. Every challenge is a chance to grow, improve, and innovate, and every setback is an opportunity to pivot. Maintain a positive outlook. Difficulties you face in life can ultimately lead you to achieve success and personal growth. The entrepreneurial journey is not for the faint-hearted, but for those who dare to dream and create and have the courage to persevere, the rewards can be extraordinary.

Corporates, startups, founders, entrepreneurs must empower their employees by providing opportunities for independent decision-making and using creativity. Encourage teamwork, facilitate clear and open communication, ensure access to the right tools, and resources to function at their best, allow flexibility at work, enable effective leaders who lead by example, provide competitive compensation, and enable opportunities for growth.

The strength of any organization lies in the collective empowerment of its workforce. As you embark on your startup journey, prioritize the well-being and growth of your team. Create a culture where innovation flourishes, collaboration thrives, and each member feels valued. By doing so, you not only build a successful enterprise but also contribute to the personal and professional fulfillment of those who make it all possible.

Being physically fit helps us endure challenges and face daily demands, while mental strength supports a positive mindset and helps us adapt to tough situations. Family provides emotional support and encouragement that boosts our confidence and determination. Together, they create a strong foundation for personal and professional growth and help us achieve lasting and fulfilling success.

I've shared my heart, my insights, and my journey with you. I hope my experiences, struggles, and stories of resilience have the power to inspire and uplift you. I want to express my gratitude for joining me on this journey through the ups and downs of my startup life. Your determination to seek knowledge and overcome obstacles is a testament to your entrepreneurial spirit. Stay curious, stay persistent, and, above all, keep believing in your vision.

As you move forward, remember that you're not alone. Seek support, learn from others, and continue to adapt. Your journey is a story waiting to be written, and I have confidence that it will be a story of triumph. Here's to your success!

www.ingramcontent.com/pod-product-compliance
Lightning Source LLC
Chambersburg PA
CBHW022001150726
47990CB00002B/545